Ralph Waldo Emerson, Charles Johnson Woodbury

Talks with Ralph Waldo Emerson

Ralph Waldo Emerson, Charles Johnson Woodbury

Talks with Ralph Waldo Emerson

ISBN/EAN: 9783337084226

Printed in Europe, USA, Canada, Australia, Japan

Cover: Foto ©ninafisch / pixelio.de

More available books at **www.hansebooks.com**

TALKS WITH

RALPH WALDO EMERSON

TALKS WITH

RALPH WALDO EMERSON

BY

CHARLES J. WOODBURY

LONDON
KEGAN PAUL, TRENCH, TRÜBNER & CO., Lᴛᴅ.
1890

TO THE YOUTH OF THE LAND
WHO ASPIRE.

I BELIEVE you will find herein the person of him whom you have never seen, but who may have been to you already a good genius, and taken an unshared place.

Take his words to me as what he would have said to you.

CHARLES J. WOODBURY.

OAKLAND, CALIFORNIA.

NOTE TO THE ENGLISH EDITION.

As it was from the youth of England, in those forepassed years whose generation will remember him, that Mr. Emerson received what he regarded the choicest compliment of his life, there is propriety in conveying to them this narration of the manner of man he was. Moreover, perspective may correct chromatic tendencies in a lens subject to aberration on account of the tender and tranquil fervour with which we regard his undiminished name, and which is quite the same on the confines of this farther sea as on his own Atlantic.

CONTENTS.

MEETING.

TALKS WITH
RALPH WALDO EMERSON.

MEETING.

WILLIAMSTOWN, Massachusetts, the home of Williams College, is an ideal village. Here one afternoon in the early autumn of 1865 arrived Ralph Waldo Emerson, unheralded by even so much as a paragraph in the county newspaper.

As Mr. Emerson was to lecture the same evening, the situation was awkward. But he soon was made aware that the group of students, to whose importunity he had listened in coming, possessed enthusiasm, even if they lacked experience ; for at once there was a stir. Within two hours, our most spacious assembly-room, the Methodist meeting-house, was procured. Placards overflowed the regular college bulletin boards, and blistered every available place, even trespassing upon

such respected preserves as the chapel,
library doors, and the fence about the
residence of Dr. Hopkins, president of the
college. Numbers of us ran from house to
house notifying their inhabitants; while
others rang the college and church bells,
unconsciously imitating Henry D. Thoreau
on an occasion somewhat similar, years before,
in Concord. That night all seats were filled.

The next morning we waited upon Mr.
Emerson with a proposition to give us some
more lectures. He consented; and so the
acquaintance of a day was lengthened into
a week. Afterward, lectures were under-
taken in North Adams, Pittsfield, and other
nigh places. When arranging for these, I
learned that, while our offence had been
venial, the manner of our atoning for it was
too declarative; for the employment of either
a local agent or preliminary printer's ink was
not permitted. Nor did it appear that his
audiences at all suffered through these omissions; for rumour of his nearness was quick
to penetrate these neighbourhoods, and his
advent was like the avatar of a master to his
communion.

My association with these appearances
necessarily threw me with Mr. Emerson.

From the first he had encouraged me, and his instruction substituted for the time that of the College. Nor did he abate his fatherly manner and interest after I had achieved a beard, but was unalterably kind for the five years after that I occasionally met him.

Thus much for these external matters that are but of interest to show my right to speak. From him, I have no right. Mr. Emerson had never a thought of, and, *à fortiori*, gave no permission for this publication. And yet it is certain that I betray nothing and violate no spirit of confidence. Every intercourse carries experience and words that are not renewable. A few of Mr. Emerson's by their own weight and personality sought depths whence they could not emerge. These would only gratify the inquisition of the curious, and belong to the domain of silence. It is the broad and human tone which makes the uncommon man interesting to us and desired by us. Conspicuously was this the case with Mr. Emerson, because it was the tone he habitually employed. It is true he was aware, especially during our earlier association, that I was in the habit of preserving his speech; and once when I remarked that it ought to have a larger public, he answered that there should be among all who would "ascend, a helpful companionship; and that which is really a good for one will be so for more." This is illustrative of his attitude which constitutes my sanction. I have written for love's sake, and that of gratitude; and I believe he would have me give to others that which was most generous and helpful to me.

The fact is, he had nothing to withhold, and generally addressed me as if I were wholly impersonal, a sort of invisible audience (an absence from the spectrum wholly desirable now); and it was not like him to be exclusive, provided his reproduction preserved accuracy and faithfulness.

About this, happily, there is little doubt. At one and twenty, the emotions are not encysted : and so little was containment possible, that I found myself in the intervals of our meetings reviving their transports. I was delighted to discover that his language came back to me without loss or change. It seemed as if my pen was a reed, through which breathed upon the paper his monologue, with the physical impression of his accent, dress, gait, and manner. And so the boy's journals are themselves a curiosity to

the unreceptive man of forty-five. Mr.
Emerson always talked slowly, and his words
had the trick of impressing themselves which
belongs to happy selection ; but it was mainly
because his speech was so wise and sincere,
and came from the depths of his own heart,
that it has sunken so deep into mine. From
some such cause, and from some such habit
of immediate revival, may it not have been
that the two contemporary gospel writers
were able to reproduce the words of Jesus?)

It has been impossible, of course, to print
these and the subsequent records as they
stand. To do so would create confusion, for
conversations are not methodical ; and, in so
long a period and to an uninformed youth,
many subjects would be discoursed upon
more than once. The reader, therefore, will
not expect to come upon the statements in
their succession.

Moreover, I have attempted a slight ar-
rangement of the subjects, which has necessitated separations and associations. But
this is all ; and no transposition has been
permitted when to do so would affect the
primitive meaning and intention. Sometimes these are obscure, and once or twice
the speaker has anticipated or quoted

himself. But even here, the words being
invariably authentic, I have refrained from
the annotating pencil, preferring to let them
stand, bethinking myself that it would be his
way. The address is to an audience which
will come to just comparisons and conclu-
sions, and recognize that the object is less to
give a bundle of reminiscences than a new
view of the man himself.

I hope no reader will feel that the contents
transgress the title. Much that a man says
is unspoken, and yet is essentially his intercourse, and not to be suppressed. Where-
fore, I bring, in the concluding chapters,
memories of air and manner; such suggestions of personality as accompanied Mr.
Emerson's words; and the effects of his fine
contagion on one who had neither theories
or prepossessions. These immediate and
inevitable impressions, made by his contact,
illustrated by his own words, are they not
still his breath in the lute, still his silent
talks?

It remains, perhaps, to explain the man-
date for these loitering memories. Why are
they ushered so late or at all? I hope they
will tell their own story and furnish adequate

reason. But some word of apology seems
appropriate, especially when so recently Mr.
Edward Emerson has delighted us with his
gift obtainable from no other, and what
must ever be regarded *the* official and
authentic life of Emerson (Cabot's) has been
published — a work beyond comparison,
genuine, copious, satisfying, and which
justifies the wise choice of its subject. Conceived in his own society, it has been
executed with marvellous fidelity to his wish
and spirit, and reproduces with exactness his
firm and sincere accent, impressive by contrast with the vague and extreme language
of too many of his followers and interpreters
when speaking of him. One feels that the
book would have his endorsement, and it
could have no higher. The portrait is gladly
and thankfully accepted as the most faithful
of all of those which have been painted by
so many loving hands. It is, perhaps, less a
portrait than a photograph. The high stature
is present, the figure and the lineaments, but
are there not absent a colour and warmth ?
Somehow it seems as if we miss the light that
drew us to him (but it is less for his sake
than ours that it is supplied)—as if the Emerson we knew has been foreign to his bio-

grapher, and could not be gathered from his posthumous papers.

Though he was inapt to distinguish between his hearers (being concerned mainly with his own thought), yet it was not possible for him to be the same to his equals in age and experience that he would be to a young man of limited knowledge of life. His memoirists have given what they got—stores, nurture, education, example. But his gift to us, while still embracing these, was something deeper. He did not so much bring facts and experiences as he became himself fact and experience to us, entering into the source of life, and penetrating at once the region of motive.

From his neighbourhood, one always returned reinvigorated, with choice moods, and sometimes even ecstacies, which carried those of extreme æsthetic sympathies and deficient ratiocinative powers quite off their feet. He knew well the wearying and prostrating moments that assault and often destroy intellectual life at its very birth, the haunting longing and aspirations, the vague unrest and insurrections which characterize the passage forth from immaturity; and he condensed the vapour into rain. His pre-

sence broke the shards of the will and concentrated the man. Nothing came afterwards
precisely as it had come before ; and our
new eyes saw that things are not entitled to
respect simply because they are. It may be
that too often the old became obsolete, but
this could be corrected. With his coming,
adolescence ended and virility began. He
aroused the best elements of the soul, agitated
it to its depth, and precipitated all it had of
intellectual principle. He first taught us to
think, and who can forget the opener of
that door ? The dawn of life to the mind—is
there a greater boon one human being can
receive from another ? Is there one like
unto it, except the dawn of love to the heart ?
Acquisitions, knowledge, training, even, can
only assume a place after it. Liberty radiated
from his presence. Then every interview
was an emancipation. Especially, can any
personality be imagined more irritating and
urging to the young and arable mind ?

So it is a youth's experience of Mr. Emerson that I would give to youth. It may be
that I am too much tethered by these strong
early associations ; that foreign and maturer
experiences may insist that he came particularly to them (as each of Vishnu's sixteen

thousand wives believed the god was peculiarly hers alone); but to me it has grown
plainer all these years that there was a divine
appointment in the recording of these talks
to a youth, that he *belonged* to the young
men. They were the natural vehicle of his
spirit; they always largely made up his
audiences, and replenished them when they
were low;. they were ever ready to second
him, soonest to greet and warmest to praise
his latest deliverance; they opened the
Divinity Schools for him when elders would
have held them closed; they supported
The Dial most eagerly, and gladly followed
further the brilliant heresiarch, his own hair
not yet gray. How many of his addresses
were delivered before colleges to which he
was constantly summoned from New England
and Virginia to the farther West, during the
years 1837 to 1879?

Amusing yet illustrative are the words of
the Worcester, Massachusetts, youth—

" We ought to go and hear such a man as
that, just to encourage him."

And I remember those winter night rides
of the Harvard students to his open evenings.
So all young men heard him greedily, insti-
gated and supported his Apprentices', Uni-

versity, theological and literary lecturing both
at home and abroad, finally culminating in
the invitation of the Independents of Glasgow
inviting him to accept the candidature for the
Lord Rectorship, and polling for him five
hundred votes.

His spirit of kinship to all young manhood
breathed from his person in public and
vitalized his page.   And he recognized it.
His feelings were invariably clear and just
to his " brave young men," his "nigh starving
youth," and "heroic boys," as he called
them.   " I cannot easily say no to them," he
said ; and so he wrote from England to Miss
Hoar—

" I have, however, some *youthful* corre-
spondents—you know my failing—friendly
young gentlemen, in different parts of
Britain."

And to Miss Peabody—

" My special parish is young men inquiring
their way of life."

And to Carlyle—

" As usual, at this season of the year, I,
incorrigible spouting Yankee, am writing an
oration to deliver to the boys in one of the
little country colleges, nine days hence.
[" The Method of Nature," before the Society·

of the Adelphi, Waterville College, Maine,
August 11, 1841.] You will say I do not
deserve the help of any Muse. Oh, if you
knew how natural it is to me to run to these
places! Besides, I always am lured on by
the hope of saying something which shall
stick by the good boys."

Even up to the confines of age, when he
receded into the shadow of its eclipse, and
when an increased desire to economize the
time as it grew short, and to mint some of
the metal so slowly hoarded, interrupted the
tranquillity with which he had been accustomed to give himself to all comers, and he
was compelled to refuse admittance to
philosophers and savants, some of whom
had journeyed a long way to see him, he did
not deny himself to young men. Then, as
always, he was to them, it is admitted,
uniformly open and kindly. He may have
declined exhausting interviews with manhood
and age coming to compare, to judge, or to
criticize ; and with lotophagi whose dream
he had no longer the energy to awaken.
But to youth there was due this larger loyalty
of sympathy. He knew what he was to
them. They held one another. So has he
not come to all who have life to seek, spirits

of the morning sort everywhere, and carried
them whither they would not have found the
way?

Well do I remember his tender, shrewd,
wise face, as I first saw it in that summer
now so long ago that one might grow from
child to manhood, which was not like any
other, because it brought me to face my own
penury, and to translate my own enigmas.
Almost before we were alone he had made
me forget in whose presence I stood. He
was merely an old, quiet, modest gentleman,
pressing me to a seat near him, and all at
once talking about college matters, the new
gymnasium, the Quarterly; and from these
about books and reading and writing; and
all as if he continually expected as much as
he gave. I, wonted to the distance demanded by the College Faculty, found it
difficult to understand this. I regarded it as
a trait of first meeting, and was prepared for
it to disappear. But the next day, on our
walk to Greylock and the Berkshire hills, the
same heartiness and sympathy inspired his
ways. And so it was ever after—no cir-
cumstances so varying, but, whether I saw
him alone or in the presence of others,
there was the ever ready welcome shining in

his eyes, the same manifest gentleness and
persistent preference of others, even hired
strangers.

I remember one day, visiting the Natural
Bridge near North Adams, Massachusetts, we
employed an old man who lived in the vicinity
as a guide, and I could not but notice how
kind and gracious and ready to serve Mr.
Emerson was—the same flavour of look,
accent, and phrase which I noticed in his
conversation with the College Professors.   It
came from the heart of the man.   While we
were under the peculiar formation called
"The Causeway," I remarked, as indicative
of the radical nature of my companion, how
indefatigably he examined the quality and
strata of the rock to determine its comparative
age, and the thoroughness with which he
studied every fissure, even down to the beryl
and emerald pools at the base of the cliff;
as if, indeed, he were soon to be called upon
to make a report about it.   He could not
take even a walk superficially.   But while he
was mastering the bridge's simple secrets, he
listened to the old guide's garrulous talk about
his own needs, and was soon telling him of a
person living two miles away who probably
could furnish the desired occupation.

"You must know him," Mr. Emerson said; and, taking a slip of paper, he wrote a note to his friend, and gave it to our new acquaintance, who then expressed a desire to see his benefactor after the presentation of the note, fearful that the call might not prove successful.

"Very well," was the reply; "my day is for you after one o'clock any time next week."

And so from others whom I have met, who knew him, I have learned how many lives he thus piloted to gift-bringing natures; how constantly he followed this practice of acquainting himself with the needs (not desires) of persons, and then bringing them together for mutual advantage.

In my own case his kindly craft won the heart first. The encouraging eyes must have seen during our earlier days together so many ill weeds; but he seemed unconscious of them. How long it was after our first greeting, and after what personal effluence in gradual talk and delightful reminiscence that one day he fell to it; and, beginning with a lecture on composition, which was a clean departure from the instructions which the Professors of Rhetoric had been giving us for two years, ended with words which showed me the light of his life!

COUNSEL.

COUNSEL.

[Although given here as one interview, the reader
will understand that it was not. The conversation
dealt with Counsel, but I have gathered here *everything* that Mr. Emerson said of that nature.]

IT was in my own room that, glancing up at
some "Laws of Writing" * on the wall, he
began abruptly—

"A sensibility to the beautiful and a passion for its forms cause such a stirring in
some men that they seek to reproduce what
they have seen. This is the attitude of art.
It has various modes of expression. Painting, statuary, music, translate readily. The

---

* It may not be amiss to reproduce here such of
these "Laws" as received Mr. Emerson's approval :—

I. Write not at all unless you have something new.

II. Write *it*, and not before, behind, and about it.

III. Have nothing of plan visible—no firstly, or
secondly, or thirdly. Show the body, not the liga-
ments.

IV. Do no violence to words. Use them etymologically.

song is the music and poem combined.
Composition is less natural. Its symbols are
arbitrary and artificial. This makes it exacting. Composition should stand at the apex
in a pyramid of mental gymnastics.

" The most interesting writing is that which
does not quite satisfy the reader. Try and
leave a little thinking for him; that will be
better for both. The trouble with most
writers is, they spread too thin. The reader
is as quick as they; has got there before, and
is ready and waiting. A little guessing does
him no harm, so I would assist him with
no connections. If *you* can see how the
harness fits, he can. But make sure that you
see it.

" Then you should start with no skeleton
or plan. The natural one will grow as you
work. Knock away all scaffolding. Neither
have exordium or peroration. What is it you
are writing for, any way? Because you have
something new to say? It is the test of the
universities, and I am glad you have made it
yours. We don't want pulse with no legumes.
To make anew and not from others is a
grand thing. You can always tell when the
thing is new; it speaks for itself. And even
among the unlettered, it declares well enough

and strong enough. From this is the projection of idioms. But add *true*, and make sure of this. Without such sanction, no one should write.

"Then what is it? Say it! Out with it! Don't lead up to it! Don't try to let your hearer down from it. That is to be commonplace. *Say* it with all the grace and force you can, and stop. Be familiar only with good expressions. Speak in your own natural way. Then, and then only, can you be interesting. Let your treatise be yourself, so your friends will say, ' —— wrote that.'

"Expression is the main fight. Search unweariedly for that which is exact. Do not be dissuaded. You say, know words etymologically. Yes, pull them apart; see how they are made; and use them only where they fit. Avoid adjectives. Let the noun do the work. The adjective introduces sound, gives an unexpected turn, and so often mars with an unintentional false note. Most fallacies are fallacies of language. Definitions save a deal of debate.

"Neither concern yourself about consistency. The moment you putty and plaster your expressions to make them hang together, you have begun a weakening process. Take

it for granted the truths will harmonize; and
as for the falsities and mistakes, they will
speedily die of themselves.   If you *must* be
contradictory, let it be clean and sharp as
the two blades of scissors meet.

"Are your theses given, or do you select?
It is well enough rarely for practice to treat
on a suggested subject.   But such writing is
at its origin derived and a peril.   Out of
your own self should come your theme; and
only thus can your genius be your friend.
Eloquence, by which I mean a statement so
luminous as to render all others unnecessary,
is only possible on a self-originated subject.

"Don't run after ideas.   Save and nourish
them, and you will have all you should entertain.   They will come fast enough, and keep
you busy.

"Reading is closely related to writing.
While the mind is plastic there should be
care as to its impressions.   The new facts
should come from nature, fresh, buoyant,
inspiring, exact.   Later in life, when there is
less danger of imitating those traits of expression through which information has been
received, facts may be gleaned from a wider
field.   But now you shall not read these
books "—pointing—" Prescott or Bancroft or

Motley. Prescott is a thorough man. Bancroft reads enormously, always understands his subject. Motley is painstaking, but too mechanical. So are they all. Their style slays. Neither of them lifts himself off his feet. They have no lilt in them. You noticed the marble we have just seen? You remember that marble is nothing but crystallized limestone? Well, some writers never get out of the limestone condition. Be airy. Let your characters breathe from you. Walk upon the ground, but not to sink. It is a fine power, this. Some men have it, prominently the French. How it manifests itself in Montaigne, especially Cotton's translation, and in Urquhart's 'Rabelais'! Grimm almost alone of the Germans has it; Borrow had it; Thoreau had it; and James Wilson—sometimes.

" Keep close to realities. Then you accustom yourself to getting facts at first hand. If we could get all our facts so, there would be no necessity for books; but they give us facts, if we know how to use them; they are the granaries of thought as well.

" Read those men who are not lazy; who put themselves into contact with the realities. So you learn to look with your eyes too.

And do not forget the Persian, Parsee, and Hindoo religious books—the Avesta, Vendidad, and the rest ; books of travel, too. And when you travel, describe what you see. That will teach you what to see. Read those who wrote about facts from a new point of view. The atmosphere of such authors helps you, even if the reasoning has been a mistake ; such a book as ' Vestiges of Creation,' for instance.

" For later philosophical studies, I would recommend writers like Bacon and Berkeley. They have been friends to me. I see you have Sharon Turner. He is a thorough-going man, and you may trust him, even when he talks with no authority save his own. Plutarch, of course, you know. And there is Darwin ! I am glad to see him here. And you must read George Borrow's book about the gypsies. [I think he meant " Lavengro."] He went among them, lived among them, and was a gypsy himself. There is nothing from second sources, nor any empiricism in his book. You can rely upon everything, and it is quaintly told. From such as he you learn not to stop until you encounter the fact with your own hand ; to search by all shows, and learn just how it

stands. Though the reward of the market is
in the thing done, the true reward is in the
doing.

"Avoid all second-hand borrowing books—
'Collections of ——,' 'Beauties of ——,' etc.
I see you have some on your shelves. I
would burn them. No one can select the
beautiful passages of another for you. It is
beautiful for him—well! Another thought,
wedding your aspirations, will be the thing
of beauty to you. Do your own quarrying.

"Do not attempt to be a great reader, and
read for facts and not by the bookful. You
must know about ownership in facts. What
another sees and tells you is not yours, but
his. If you had seen it, you would not have
seen what he did, and, even less, what he
tells. Your only relief is to find out all you
can about it, and look at it in all possible
lights. Keep your eyes open and see all you
can; and when you get the right man, question him close. So learn to divine books, to
feel those that you want without wasting much
time over them. Remember you must know
only the excellent of all that has been presented. But often a chapter is enough. The
glance reveals when the gaze obscures. Some-
where the author has hidden his message.

Find it, and skip the paragraphs that do not talk to you."

Upon my pressing him for directions more particular and practical, a process which was rarely successful—he hated details, and avoided them—he, after a moment's hesitation, continued as follows :—

"Well, learn how to tell from the beginnings of the chapters and from glimpses of the sentences whether you need to read them entirely through. So turn page after page, keeping the writer's thought before you, but not tarrying with him, until he has brought you to the thing you are in search of; then dwell with him, if so be he has what you want. But recollect you only read to start your own team.

"Newspapers have done much to abbreviate expression, and so to improve style. They are to occupy during your generation a large share of attention. [This was said nearly a quarter of a century ago. It was as if he saw ahead the blanket editions.] And the most studious and engaged men can only neglect them at his cost. But have little to do with them. Learn how to get *their* best too, without their getting yours. Do not read them when the mind is creative.

And do not read them thoroughly, column
by column. Remember they are made for
everybody, and don't try to get what is not
meant for you.) The miscellany, for instance,
should not receive your attention. There is
a great secret in knowing what to keep out
of the mind as well as what to put in. And
even if you find yourself interested in the
selections, you cannot use them, because the
original source is not of reference. You
cannot quote from a newspaper. Like some
insects, it died the day it was born. The
genuine news is what you want, and practice
quick searches for it. Give yourself only
so many minutes for the paper. Then you
will learn to avoid the premature reports and
anticipations, and the stuff put in for people
who have nothing to think.

"Reading long at one time anything, no
matter how it fascinates, destroys thought
as completely as the inflections forced by
external causes. Do not permit this. Stop
if you find yourself becoming absorbed, at
even the first paragraph. Keep yourself out
and watch for your own impressions. This
is one of the norms of thought. And you
will accumulate facts in proportion as you
become a fact. Otherwise you will accumu-

late dreams. Information is nothing, but the man behind it.

"So you cannot make too much of yourself. It is all there is of you. How many do you know who are made up mainly of fragments of others? But follow your own star, and it will lead you to that which none other can attain. Imitation is suicide. You must take yourself for better or for worse as your portion. A man can only get an extemporized half-possession of another's gift; and what came wholly natural from him has, in spite of the best grace and skill, an impertinent air from the borrower. The elder sentiment will not thus keep the elder fire.

"I commiserate any one who is subject to the misery of being overplaced. What he is stands over him and thunders, and denies what he says. Assist this tendency which nothing can defeat. Yield not one inch to all the forces which conspire to make you an echo. That is the sin of dogmatism and creeds. Avoid them; they build a fence about the intellect.

"You are anxious about your career. I know without your telling me. Every college boy is. You think you can study out yourself what you are best fitted for? No.

But you remember our *séance* with Professor
——, over in the chemical laboratory yester-
day; how he took a substance and tried it
with others, one after another, until he discovered the affinity? So a man finds by
trying what he can do best. Each man and
woman is born with an aptitude to do something impossible to any other. Here on your
shelf is Fénélon. Who can make his pale
Fenelonism but he?

" By working, doing for others simul-
taneously with the doing of your own work,
you make the greatest gain. That is the
generous giving or losing of your life which
saves it. Don't put this aside until you are
more at liberty. That is slow death. Have
something practical on your hands, it makes
small matter what, at once. If your disposition is right you will select well. Turn
to the first thing that comes to hand and do
it. It is a great thing to get into the habit
of doing all things thoroughly. By-and-by
one discovers that he has done one thing
better than his mates; and soon it is plain
· that there is one thing which he alone can do.
And action is the natural and noble expression of thought, its *chef d'œuvre ;* it is always
to be preferred. Make certain that you have

yours—not something, but your own. Do you
remember the story among the legends of
Arthur about the witch who was brewing
the liquid which should open the eyes of all
the people? How some drops spattered into
the eyes of the serving-boy, who thereupon
incontinently fled, divining that he was to be
slain? Were all eyes anointed, how many
would be kept on one's own pot? So live
in a clean and clear loyalty to your own
affair. Do not let another's, no matter how
attractive, tempt you away. Then true and
surprising revelations come to you, and
experiences resembling the manifestations of
genius; the first characteristic of which is
veracity; the second, surprise; the third,
spontaneity; the fourth, sensibility to the
laws of the universe. Genius can see the
event as well in front as behind; it tells
where the city ought to stand as well before
as after it is built.

"And to build the city is the great
accomplishment, not to possess it. There
are so many who are content to be without
being anything. Opportunities approach
only those who use them. Even thoughts
cease by-and-by to visit the idle and "—after
a pause—" the perverse. But sudden and un-

foreseen helps and continued encouragement
are vouchsafed to the devout worker. For
God is everywhere, having His will, and He
cannot be baffled. Make His business yours,
as did His son. The man who works with
Him is constantly assured of achievement
and the melioration of the race. Such
equipment the scholar needs.

"Be choice in your friendships. You can
have but few, and the number will dwindle
as you grow older. Select minds who are
too strong and large to pretend to knowledge
and resources they do not really possess.
They address you sincerely."

As he rose to go, we saw from the little
door of the Hermitage * the spire of the
chapel in the gathering dark.

"How many faiths are there in this
village?" he asked, as he descended the
steps.

Before I could reply, trying to call to mind
the number of churches, I heard his quiet
voice again—

* There was near the rear of Professor Albert
Hopkins' garden an isolated, octagon-shaped, brick
structure formerly used as a magnetic observatory,
but in my time known as the "Hermitage," and
rented by the college to any student who would
occupy it.

"Three thousand, five hundred people; three thousand, five hundred faiths in the village of Williamstown ! Let yours not come from tradition. Life is awry at best. The effort should be evermore to widen the circle, so as to admit ventilation. Seek first spirit, and second spirit, and third and evermore spirit !"

About poetry he uttered the following suggestions, occasioned by the criticism of some Class-day rhymes :—

" I suppose you read your verses over after they are written ? "

" Generally."

" I suppose, then, after a little they grow old to you ? "

" Indeed, they do."

"And you continue to write. If after a long time you look any of your lines over, and you come to one, or a succession, and say to yourself, 'That is good,' it is good ; but destroy everything from which this verdict must be withheld. The ' me ' is the judge, after all ; and if a thing seems good to me, it shall to my fellows. I can sympathize with the desire for outward confirmation ; still, the poet is his own assurance ; he shall be conscious of himself. If you

have a sensitive and poetic soul, thank God
for it. It is not yours, save as a gift. The
highest and truest utterances of the poet are
not his. Poetry," and here he lapsed into
that manner of reverie as if all hearers were
far away, "whether it comes in dreams or in
gleams, is noble. It must serve no sordid
uses; it is of the above."

Then, after a pause—

" Did I not see Montaigne among your
books the other day? You shall not read
Montaigne and be a poet.

"You must keep some fact-books for poetry.
I think that they are much more nearly related
to poetry than rhyme or rhythm. Study
Greek for expression; but the poetic *fact* is
half the battle. Nature, gathered in by the
sensitive soul, forms the furniture of the poet.
Look out at this Indian summer. There is
something hygienic in the blue of it; it is
the mountains' own colour. Every place has
its air. From the locality of Rome, for
instance, emanates such an air that the finest
men grow inspired by it, and want to live
there always.

" Did you ever think about the logic of
stimulus? Nature supplies her own. It is
astonishing what she will do, if you give her

a chance. In how short a time will she
revive the over-tired brain ! A breath under
the apple-tree, a siesta on the grass, a whiff
of wind, an interval of retirement, and the
balance and serenity are restored. A clean
creature needs so little and responds so
readily ! There is something as miraculous as
the gospels in it. Later in life, society becomes a stimulus. Occasionally, the gentle
excitation of a cup of tea is needed. A mind
invents its own tonics, by which, without permanent injury, it makes rapid rallies and
enjoys good moods. Conversation is an
excitant, and the series of intoxications it
creates is healthful. But tobacco, tobacco—
what rude crowbar is that with which to pry
into the delicate tissues of the brain ! "

Years after, I met Mr. Emerson in the
West, and mentioned in the conversation a
bit of exciting experience among the Ten-
nessee mountains, which drew from him the
following—

"What tonic can be more inspiriting and
healthful than an adventure ? It gives back
to the blood all its youth."

CRITICISM

CRITICISM.

A GROUP of students were in the habit of assembling in one of the larger college-rooms for purposes of practice in debate ; and one afternoon Mr. Emerson came quietly in (but not without having been solicited time and again). He refused to permit the discussion to stop, but, seating himself on a sofa, he gave straight attention to the speakers. It was our custom to appoint at the beginning of each session a critic to perform at its close the duties indicated by the name. After the abbreviated exercises were ended, at our intercession, Mr. Emerson, from his seat, offered some comment, ending in the announcement of certain laws of criticism which undoubtedly prescribed his own attitude and method.

I well remember the shrewd listening that his opening words disclosed. How surprised we were to hear him even repeat the names of two or three (of previous acquaintance with him, however) who had spoken after his arrival !

" Why should not," he asked, "advantages be bartered like commodities? You have sufficient for all your speeches if they are rightly distributed. Let A—— purchase a little fluency from B——, and C—— some earnestness from X——, who might make a good investment by securing a bit of A——'s spare accuracy. If this could be accomplished, and B—— and C—— exchange, the one a little logic for the other's abundant energy, you would have a most excellent debate."

After a few words more in the same humorous and good-natured strain, he continued more gravely—

"I was interested in your critic's report. But there are nine of you here; then there should be nine critics. It is possible that you associate a wrong meaning with this word. I observed that your critic noted such minutiæ as that a certain word was pronounced wrong; that a plural verb followed a single nominative; that a gesture was made with the index finger instead of the open hand; that a speaker stood with his feet six inches apart instead of two. So you regard the speeches as so many targets, and listen to pick flaws, to find faults and little inaccuracies. You gain something in marking these things alone, but you lose immensely more. Criticism should not imply to you such a watching out, for that begets hostility of thought, a closing of the mind to the natural impulsions of the speech, lest it be influenced by them; and indulgence in the silent rehearsing of premature rejoinders. You are chiefly here, I take it, for the study of method, manner, style; then you should project yourselves into sympathy with the speaker; make certain that you receive his effort; receive it all, and receive it well; put yourself in his place; try and see why he sees as he does; and then proceed outward to investigate his sentiments and their expression. Remember, all criticism dealing with isolated points is superficial. The prevailing thought and disposition are your main care.

"Then seek what is characteristical. Get the method of the man; the way in which he tries to develop and impress his idea. Attend closely to the *quality* of the matter presented. It is an index of the speaker's originality and culture, and therefore of his ability to impress others.

"When your attention is held without effort from yourself; when you are conscious of thoughtfulness, a change of opinion working within—then attend, attend. Your speaker has power. Overlook all fault, intonation, emphasis, pronunciation. Lay hold of his secret. The genuine impressions of a speech are the thoughts it immediately arouses, and these are the sources of true critical activity!"

I do not think of Mr. Emerson as primarily a critic. His was not generally the posture indicated by the word. He was familiar with the laws that determine excellence of form, but sincerity and the satisfaction of the moral sense constituted his criterion.

"The first and main attention of men to one another is to listen and be taught," he said; "and we are continually surprised at the riches of our fellows."

For this satisfaction, and not as a condition of criticism, he accorded full reception, and gave himself without reservation; and so, when he chose to exercise it—and perhaps there were few varieties of intellectual play he enjoyed better—he had a large advantage in the feat of mere criticism; for he contained his subjects; he felt their limit and atmosphere, and all that he said showed with a

fine clarity that he fully interpreted and defined
them. Moreover, he had the habit of justice;
was never the least equivocal, self-interested,
or dictated to by party. His high moral intelligence enabled him to point out the real
meanings and issues below the surface of
prominent but transient emergencies and
events. Of consequence, his historical and
biographical judgments have only been
affected by the discovery of facts and perspective unknown to him. He always saw the
good—a rare trait; it is easy to point out
defects.

He was not capable of cynicism, nor was
he acerb. Even when provocation was great,
his satire was so gentle and genial that it
warmed even its object. He did not correct
slips made in his presence. When he was
less abstinent, the occasion plainly demanded
it, as when, with pleasant emphasis, he reminded a student who spoke of his reference
to the *mu*seum that he accented the second
syllable instead of the first.

Mr. Emerson talked apparently without
reservation to me about his contemporaries
and historical personages. In this and the
succeeding chapter I select such of his
delightful comment as seems distinguished

for the consideration of "his noble young men."

I remember one afternoon we were walking among the hills of Williamstown in the locality known as Bryant's Glen. At every little space, some new aspect of scenery invited pause. The landscape was one apt to suggest to such a youth as Bryant was at eighteen the " Thanatopsis." We saw at a little distance across the sward the ravine creeping out of the swath of sunshine between the ragged hills into its own dark and tangled fragment of forest. In the immediate nook where he wrote his poem the scattered trees are of shrunken shaft, like a life which ends without accomplishment.

"Yonder is a serious mountain," said Mr. Emerson, pointing to Greylock. " I should think this would be just the place to read 'The Excursion.' The hills are very like those of Westmoreland. Here one can see the poet, standing on the shore and looking off on the wide sea-light, and backward on the glows of the mountains, and then recognizing the inner supernal light, the subjective, as he framed that most celebrated combination—

"' The light which never was on sea or land,
    The inspiration and the poet's dream.'

"Wordsworth," he continued, pronouncing
the name as if it were spelled Waurdsworth,
"is the poet of England. I see the *Reader*
lately acknowledges it. He is the only one
who comes up to high-water mark. No
mannerism in him! Other poets start out
with a theory which dwarfs or distorts them ;
he was careful to have none. Other writers
have to affect what to him, thus, is natural.
So they have what Arnold called *simplism*,
he, simplicity. His attorney wished him to
go to law with Lord ——, to recover his estate
of which that peer had defrauded him.
Wordsworth refused, saying, 'No ; I must not
forget it is my profession to write poetry.'
And so he went into the forest, and lived on
bread, and—wrote poetry. He lived very
plainly. When Scott came to see him he had
no ale to offer him or wine, and so the
novelist was wont to go to the village inn
for his daily glass of ale. And one day as, in
company with his host, he was walking by the
inn, the landlord appeared and asked Sir
Walter if he had come for his cracker and
mug of ale! Afterwards, I believe, the son
of the peer who had his estate, who was a
gentleman, compounded with the Words-
worths, and restored to them their property.

" The first three books of ' The Excursion '
are the best. The discussions are unin-
teresting, but the adventures of the wonderful Pedlar always charm me. There is
sometimes an extreme even in Wordsworth.
What is that 'horrible' line in 'Peter
Bell'?

" ' The long dry see-saw of this horrible bray.'

" The ass is unpoetical ; and perhaps Alice
Fell is too childish, a little. His sonnets are
good. They are, indeed, as pure, chaste,
transparent as Milton's. They are the
witchery of language. He is the greatest
poet since Milton."

What is it Bulwer says of Wordsworth ?

" Wordsworth's poetry is of all existing in
the world the most calculated to refine,
etherealize, to exalt ;—to offer most corre-
spondent counterpoise to the scale that
inclines to earth."

Emerson could quote almost entirely the
" Prelude " and " Excursion," so much had
he pondered them. I remember he was
abundant in reminiscences of Wordsworth
and Scott, and told me many anecdotes of
them, one or two of which are identical with
those narrated in " English Traits," only some

way they seemed to be much better told than
they are there.

"There are no books," he concluded, "for
boys, like the poems of Sir Walter Scott.
Every boy loves them if they are not put into
his hands too late. 'Marmion,' 'The Lay
of the Last Minstrel,' 'The Lady of the
Lake;' they surpass everything for boy-
reading we have."

As an amusing instance of literary repeti-
tion, he referred in this connection to the
musical lines in some elder verses of a
countryman of Scott's :—

> "Make me thy wrack
> When I come back,
> But spare me when I go,"

by comparison with lines in Martial's twenty-
fifth epigram :—

> "*Parcete dum propero,*
> *Mergite dum redeo.*"

It was uncommon to hear Mr. Emerson
speak with such emphasis of any one as he
did of Plato. At our first railroad restaurant,
where, although there was plenty of time,
everybody was eating as they do generally
at travel-tables, Mr. Emerson leaned over
toward me, and said humorously, with a
smile—

"Wasn't it Plato who said of the citizens of Agrigentum—they, you know, were colossal architects and eaters—'These people build as if they were immortal, and eat as if they were to die instantly'?"

"Read Plato's 'Republic!' Read Plato's 'Republic!' Read Plato's 'Republic!'" he repeated on another occasion. "He lifts man toward the divine, and I like it when I hear that a man reads Plato. I want to meet that man. For no man of self-conceit can go through Plato."

Carlyle, I believe, confesses that he cannot read Plato.

"I am glad you have so many of the Greek Tragedies," continued Mr. Emerson. "Read them largely and swiftly in translation, to get their movement and flow; and then a little in the original every day. For the Greek is the fountain of language. The Latin has a definite shore-line, but the Greek is without bounds." Then, after a pause, he added, half to himself, "Dead languages, called dead because they can never die."

Of Gibbon he spoke strikingly, as follows—

"He is one of the best readers that ever lived in England. You know his custom of

examining himself both before and after his
reading a book, to see what had been added
to his mental experience? All previous and
contemporary British historians are bare-
footed friars in comparison with Gibbon.
He was an admirable student, a tremendous
worker. He banished himself to a lonely
château, just to work harder; but he thought
uncleanly. He had—as also did Aristophanes, whom I never could read on that
account—an imagination degraded and never
assoiled, a low wit like that which defaces out-
buildings. He was a disordered and coarse
spirit, a mind without a shrine, but a great
example of diligence and antidote to laziness.

"Locke was a stalwart thinker. He
erected a school of philosophy which limited
everything to utility. But the soul has its
own eyes, which are made illuminating by the
Spirit of God."

With the same lofty accent he spoke of
Harriet Martineau, and compared her attitude
with that of her brother :—

" It was a grief to me when I learned that
she had become materialist." After a long
pause he added, lifting his head, " God? It
is all God."

" Read Chaucer," he said ; " in a day you

E

will get into his language, and then you will like him. Humour the lines a little, and they are full of music.

"I think I will recite a strain from his 'Good Counsel,' and, were I you, I would copy it and have it always with me. It is a scripture."

He then delivered, without hesitation, but very slowly and thoughtfully, sinking his voice at the end of every line—

" Flee from the press and dwell with soothfastness ; '
    Suffice thee thy good, though it be small ;
For hoard hath hate and climbing tickelness,
    Press hath envy and weal is blent over all,
    Savour no more than thee behove shall ;
Rule well thyself that other folk canst rede,
And truth thee shall deliver, it is no dread.

" Pain thee not each crooked to redress
    In trust of her that turneth as a ball,
Great rest stands in little business ;
    Beware also to spurn against an awl,
    Strive not as doth a croke with a wall ;
Daunte thyself that dauntest others deed,
And truth thee shall deliver, it is no dread.

" That thee is sent receive in buxomness,
    The wrestling of this world asketh a fall ;
Here is no home, here is but wilderness.
    Forth, pilgrim ! forth, beast, out of thy stall !
    Look up on high and thanke God of all ;
Waive thy lust and let thy ghost thee lead,
And truth thee shall deliver, it is no dread ! "

He repeated the last two lines, pronouncing the last word so as to rhyme with the last of the penultimate line, and then—

"I have seen an expurgated edition of Chaucer; shun it! Shun expurgated editions of any one, even Aphra Bene or François Villon. They will be expurgating the Bible and Shakspeare next."

Of Shakspeare he talked much, and always without a word of subtraction. Of no one else did he speak in a similar strain of encomium, excepting that imperial man, Walter Savage Landor; and of him Mr. Emerson had this abatement, referring to his conversation—

"He does not aspirate; drops his h's like a cockney. I cannot understand it."

He did not think that Shakspeare wrote Wolsey's soliloquy and the scene that follows it, on the ground that Shakspeare always wrote so that the thought should publish its own rhythm, a characteristic not observable, he contended, in these passages.

"So far as we know," he said, "'The Essays of Montaigne' is the only book Shakspeare owned. Like Aristophanes, Shakspeare had the care of the presentation of his plays, so they were kept practical. It has had much to do with their surviving. Whenever either got into 'the clouds,' he got down out of them as fast as he could.

"But Shakspeare was a wonder. He struck twelve every time;" and then, after a pause, "We have not such creatures in America." Somehow the words and his half sad manner in uttering them, brought back to me old Nestor's lament, "For not at any time have I seen such men, nor shall I, as Perithous and Gyas, etc."

He spoke of the songs of Ben Jonson as "the finest in the English language. They are rich and succulent and metery. Few men have that wonderful power of rhyming, especially double-rhyming, that he has;" and he instanced "The Mask of Dædalus," and recited four stanzas of Jonson's ode to himself in illustration.

I was much interested in his words on Shelley and Blake. While he seemed hesitatingly to recognize and allow the wide gleams of truth the disciples of these mystics claim for them, he yet insisted that their visions were rather a curiosity than a discovery, and rebuked them strongly for their trait of "obliteration of the imagination" by natural objects.

"I cannot read Shelley with comfort," he said. "His visions are not in accord with the facts ; they are not accurate. He soars to sink." From Blake he quoted "The Tiger"—

"Tiger, tiger, burning bright,"

over and over, almost the only thing I ever heard him quote that he put into the "Parnassus."

He criticized Tennyson as "factitious" and a "posture-master," said that his inspiration is "scanty, and does not arrive at extremities." When I reminded him that in "English Traits" he says of Tennyson, "The colour of the dawn flows over the horizon from his pencil," he answered after a moment—

"And that is true, too."

He many times referred to Leigh Hunt, and advised me to read him, "a true and gentle friend to all men."

Of Matthew Arnold he said, "He is stored with all critical faculties except humour, but so far he shows little of that." And of Browning, "He is always a teacher."

"Have you read any of Goethe?" he asked.

On my replying affirmatively as to "Wilhelm Meister," he said—

"Ah yes, that is good. It wants to be
read well; it contains the analysis of life.
Wasson, in the *Atlantic*, some time ago had
some excellent words upon it, more a pane-
gyric than a criticism. But Wasson must
have just come to it. We have loved Meister
a long time."

Of Fichte he said, "He would use any
weapon to convert a hearer. I think he
would trepan a person, if so he could pass
his own edacious conceptions into the bared
brain." In this connection he commended
the example of the German professor who
stood on his head when his audience thinned.

I once asked his opinion of the novels of
George Sand, and he answered as follows :—

"It is wonderful the amount she has
written—everything; she seems to know the
world. But her stories—I do not know about
them; I do not read stories. I never could
turn a dozen pages in 'Don Quixote' or
Dickens without a yawn. He takes too long
to tell a little; too much of a reporter who
must fill a column. Why read novels? We
meet stranger creatures than their heroes.
What writer of stories would not be derided
if he gave us creatures as impossible as Nero
or Alva or Joan of Arc?"

He frequently drew comparisons between the authors who ought to write for the good of the world and those who ought to write merely for their own good. As an instance of the latter, he mentioned a poet then rather the fashion, who had recently appeared in England.

"I was surprised," he said, "at the praise of the —— *Review*. The man had no sun— a derived light like a star's. He had read ' Festus,' and the ' Life Drama ' leaked out. It must have been inspired by a headache, the delirium of the tripod without its vati- cination ; the verses are not of the kind that the people like—nothing hearty or happy in them."

This last trait he expected in all good writing. I remember in one of our earliest interviews how he spoke of a manuscript volume of poetical studies that had then just been sent him by my friend Edward King, " They are wonderful for a boy of seventeen, but they are too melancholy. He seems to see nothing but the horrible. Now, the world is joyous. He paints every- thing in black, and yet he is a rosy-cheeked boy. I wonder at it. We cannot have the Rembrandt colour. Melancholy is unen-

durable; grief is abnormal. Victor Hugo
has written such a book. I have not read
it; I do not read the sad in literature."

These words were the first seismic tremors
in my new heavens and new earth. They
set my wits a-swimming, troubled me with
apprehension of possible limitation in him,
and finally coerced me into a collision which
I regard as ridiculous enough now, but which
my conscience will not permit me to conceal, because the experience is a valuable
object-lesson to the young men, to whom this
narrative primarily speaks; and because it
illustrates Mr. Emerson's peculiar ways with
his lovers, emancipating them by saving
them even from himself. Other readers will
not be interested in these juvenile hysterics.
After setting down in my journal his conversation for the day, I could not restrain
the expression of my doubts. As they are
necessary to a full understanding of the situation, I will venture to transcribe the passage
as follows :—

"Mr. Emerson said to-day that no one
ought to write as Hawthorne has. I did
not ask him what he meant. This is of no
use with him. He talks in riddles, or, I
should say, rebuses, so perspicuous and pic-

turesque are his words, and one has to guess
his meaning. This is not difficult often;
and to-day I am pretty sure he was referring
to the nether side of human experience com-
memorated by Hawthorne, for he spoke in
connection of King's melancholy verse, and
said he would not read 'Les Miserables'
because the subjects and treatment are not
cheerful. It cannot be that he, a guide in
morals, persistently shuts his eyes to the only
class of facts which makes morals necessary?

"He tells me to read the Eastern theological books—bibles, he calls them—and a
long and starving Ramadan have I had with
them; but how can *he* have read and endorse
them? Their inspiration is of the pall, their
language of the grave; their message, what
there is of it, is covered with vapours of the
tomb. In Saadi, Hafiz, and the rest, whom
he so warmly approves, what else is there
but the same tragic story, lightened, perhaps, with sentiment and fancy? The whole
oriental literature, so far as I know it, is an
elegy.

"In our Bible, from Moses, desolate, broken
with disappointment, and dying in despair
within sight of his unattained goal, to the

mysteries of the Revelations, there is the
same shadow of mournfulness. A bleak
wind blows through all the history of the
kings and judges; Job is the story of doubt;
Solomon shows us a brow of sorrow, a mind
strewn with shameful memories and sullen
remorse; David's psalms and those of the
other minstrels are rather the appeals of a
heart in insurrection against its own sin than
the lyric and happy exultations of a freed
and joyous spirit. Then there are the
prophets. Their very word is a 'burden;'
their thunderbolts echo from skies heavy and
black, and the lofty Ideal their lightnings
momentarily disclose is a 'Man of sorrows,
and acquainted with grief.' When he
comes—— O, the breath of the gospels,
and Paul's sorrowful eloquence after the
warning light struck home to his heart, and
the voice of the crucified one bade it lodge
there for ever! How *can* a theology or a
morality one 'shall'—to use Mr. Emerson's
own word—trust be built up and blink these
facts of the dawn of religion?

"Martyrs have given the Church its man-
liest life; so only did it become brave and
saintly.

"But I know not what to say. He 'does

not read the sad.' What is left, then? We just finished 'Agamemnon' last semester, and since then I have read ' Prometheus.' If ever a literature respired 'the sad,' surely the Greek does. There Destiny is omnipresent. Its misty fane is the only one in the countless temples whose crowd of unsacred divinities and gods makes a godless materialism that presents no obscure glimmer of hope, and is the mantle of their followers' philosophy. Lucretius, and even Plato, trace their thought as if on sable shrouds. Where is the classic tragedy that does not labour under the stress and dirge of the unlifted cloud of Fate? It makes even the comedies shudder. The poisoned chalice is borne from the Greek to the Tiber hills. Virgil betrays the chill of the 'perpetual night' of which Catullus sung. Daphne and Lalage, Chloe and Doris, with all their lilies and roses, do not lift his spirit. The worm of the grave trails over the page of Horace.

" He spoke approvingly of my portrait of Dante yonder on the wall. But what is the story of those features? They are born of night and filled with it.

" He has brought me to Chaucer. (Why did I not find him earlier?) But all the

pictures of this the father and mother spirit
are shaded with dark colours.

"Then there is Shakspeare. Master, what
has been thy coined gold of speech, so
chary with its largess, of him! But too
faithful is he to humanity to conceal its
myriad miseries, and how transparent is his
own sorrow in the sonnets?

"I wonder if he would forbid the sights
blind Milton saw? But what poems are
these—'Paradise Lost,' 'Samson Agonistes,'
and 'Il Penseroso!'

"Even among the minor poets of fancy
merely, who have not taken hold of the
gloomy mysteries of being, there is this
same woful misery. From Tibullus to Tom
Moore, the jocund chansons are twined with
the blossoms of the tomb. Anacreon knows
well of

"Death, with his head wrapped in gloom;"

Lesbia's and Sulpicia's kisses are 'mingled
with sad tears,' and their foreheads are
bowed earthward with chaplets of cypress.
I know not where, from Mrs. Hemans to
Sappho, to escape in either sex this fulness
of tearful sensibility. Think of the forms
of classic and ideal beauty wrung from

the breaking heart and too ephemeral lips of Keats !

" Ah no, Brother Moschus, you may not escape this cadence of the minor chord. Its vibration is felt in all our literature.

" There must be something deeper in all this than the effort of the mind of man in investigating the problems of his being and the unintelligible universe. May it not be that the mystery of expression, itself impenetrable and elusive, haunts with its tantalizing irony the pursuit of the unutterable secret, and results necessarily in wounded endeavour ? *Allons.*"

The next day, full of these trist thoughts, at the cost of a struggle, but with a youth's temerity, I told Mr. Emerson of my inability to accept his statements on this matter as I understood them. He heard me patiently, watched my quivering lips a moment, and then said briefly, but with beaming glance—

" Very well. I do not wish disciples." And now I see that the occurrence concealed a crisis in our affairs. For from this time disappeared in his pupil the boyish and servile acquiescence, and I doubt not in the master the feeling of nausea it could not but cause. The release saved me my friend, and made of his friendship a greater blessing ;

even as the vision came again and tarried
with the monk after he had shown himself to
be worthy of it.

This was a long step toward manhood ; but
the remarkable reply held for me a still deeper
teaching, and one yet more psychologically
formative, in that it exhibited to me the
foolish habit I had fallen into of concerning
myself with my friend's wares rather than
himself.   And afterwards I found myself less
and less drawn by Mr. Emerson's opinions,
advice, literary judgments, etc.   Not that they
did not interest me.   One would have to be
less or more than human not to respond to
these unique and wise overflowings of insight
and experience.   But now I saw there was a
far richer gift aloof from these and in reserve,
namely, the personality of the man himself.
And to all youth I would say, recognize this
in every great soul with whom you come in
contact—the power that is his that made him
what he is.   It is more to you than all his
esoteric facts and ideas.   He conveys it to
you in what he says, and in what he omits
to say ; in his laches and lapses ; and it is
his greatest gift that he has such life adequate
to survive the deadening and mechanical
processes through which he has been com-

pelled to come to you in his books and give you himself.

Of American contemporaries Mr. Emerson spoke as follows :—

"The connecting link between England and America is Oliver Wendell Holmes. If that acute-minded man had been born in England, they would never have tired of making much of him. He has the finest sensibility, and that catholicity of taste without which no large and generous nature can be developed. Everything interests him. He has phases which make him welcome as well to Bacchus as Minerva. Open to Euphrosyne? Yes, and to Eresicthon !

"James Russell Lowell is a man of wit; a genial man, of good inspirations, who can write poems of wit and something better. It does one good to read him. He has a good deal of self-consciousness, and never forgave Margaret Fuller and Thoreau for wounding it.

"'Leaves of Grass,' by Walt Whitman, is a book you must certainly read. It is wonderful. I had great hopes of Whitman until he became Bohemian. He contrasts with Poe, who had an uncommon facility for rhyme, a happy jingle. Poe might have become much had he been capable of self-direction. Thoreau was attracted to New York to see Whitman."

Mr. Emerson said this as if it were at once a compliment and endorsement, and remarked upon the attraction as being " psychological."

He spoke of Daniel Webster as " deformed. Every drop of his blood had eyes that looked downward. He knew the heroes of '76 well enough; he did not know the heroes of his own day when he met them on the streets. He became to me the type of decay. To gain his ambition, he gave ease, pleasure, happiness, wealth; and then added honour and truth. He had a wonderful intellect; but of what importance is that when the rest of the man is gone? He was oblivious of consequences, and "—after a pause—" consequently oblivion."

Of Forceythe Willson he spoke with great regret :—

" There we were," he said, " Longfellow, Whittier, Channing, all of us, writing letters to our friends in Michigan, Indiana, everywhere, to find who and where was the poet that was delighting us so ; and all the time he lived in his own hermit-hut, not a stone's throw from Mr. Lowell's house in Cambridge.

You remember his parting song? It far sur-
passes Poe in his most peculiar vein;" and
he quoted slowly :—

> " This is the burden of the heart,
>   The burden that it always bore ;
> We live to love, we meet to part,
>   And part to meet on earth no more ;
> We clasp each other to the heart,
>   And part to meet on earth no more.

> " There is a time for tears to start—
>   For dews to fall and larks to soar—
> The time for tears is when we part
>   To meet upon the earth no more.
> The time for tears is when we part
>   To meet on this wide earth—no more."

" Hawthorne was always haunted by his
ancestry, who spelt the name Hathorne.
His gait and moods were of the sea. He
had kinship to pirates and sailors. What
was it Channing wrote by inspiration from
him ?

> " ' Unceasing roll the deep green waves,
>   And crash their cannon down the sand,
>   The tyrants of the patient land,
> Where mariners hope not for graves.'

But his writings are of the terrible, the
grotesque, and sombre. There is nothing
joyous in them. It is the same way with
Hugo. No man ought to write so.

F

"Abbott wrote a pitiful book about Napoleon; but he was a wonderful man enough—always fell on his feet. The best memoirs of him are those of Leuzier. Scott is too British; O'Meara, the Irish surgeon, writes well of him—a little low, untutored, rough; but he had personal access, and Napoleon breathed through all the men about him. What was that he said about making his generals out of mud? His meanness, which could speak no chivalric word, spoke there, but it spoke fact."

Of Agassiz he quoted :—

"Nature selects some man, who is impressionable, thoughtful, simple-hearted, and conducts him softly to some one of her little closets, and bids him enter; and when he comes back, the world stands still to know what he learned there. When a created thing gets an interpreter, it crowns him."

And of Everett and Ticknor :—

"Edward Everett and George Ticknor were men especially excellent in the modern languages. The golden time of Everett's life was when he was Professor of Greek at Cambridge. He did more real good there than as senator or governor. He had a fine conception of Greece, and a genius for the

Greek language. He returned from Europe,
and was professor to the class above me
when I was a student. As a college president
he was not successful. He noticed little
things too much, as whether an undergraduate
touched his hat to him or not, and the
students hated him. Therefore he resigned."

CONCORD.

CONCORD.

SACRED village, whose every bush burns with the fire its immortals have left! Whither shall the devout pilgrim who would breathe the noblest inspirations with which the New World has yet been blessed turn, if not thither? And for the youth who would nourish his soul with high ambitions and electrify it with rare associations, is there any atmosphere like that of the revolutionary battlefield with Emerson's historic inscription,—the classic river that lisps as it flows; the hermit lake Walden; the eloquent cairn; the "wood-lots," domestic but shadowy, where the minute life celebrated by Hawthorne toils through Sisyphean days,—and all the scenes made precious by the victories they have witnessed?

Moreau's faith was in Concord. His motto was: "*Ne quid Quæsiveris extra te Concordiamque.*" But Concord in a spiritual sense is in William Ellery Channing's "Wan-

derer," and those who cannot know directly
its inspirations will find them as nearly as
such gracious influences can survive the book-
making ordeal in that little volume. Mr.
Channing *erwandert* Concord. The "old
Virginia road" was familiar with his person.
He knew even better than Thoreau the uplands'
every precinct and meadows, penetrated in
all directions the woods and groves and
marshes, rowed the ponds, and swam the
rivers. With bright humour he alludes to his
experiences : "Fatigue, blazing sun, face par-
boiled, the pint cup never scoured, shaving
unutterable, stockings dreary having taken to
peat." His descriptions were made realistic
by these daily exposures year after year,
saturated, so to say, with the sunshine and
the humidity of the Middlesex woods. Mr.
Emerson quoted to me from the "Sea Scene"
(not a portion of "The Wanderer")—

> " The purple kelp waves to and fro,
>   The white gulls, curving, scream along ;
>   They fear not thy funereal song,
>   Nor the long surf that combs to snow."

" ' The Wanderer ' is a conscientious piece
of work," he added. "It reminds me of
Concord."

Of Margaret Fuller he spoke much at one

time and another, but nothing that teaches,
unless it is the following :—

"I was amused with what she said of
Bettine Brentano—something like this : 'She
has not pride enough. Only when I am
sure of myself would I pour out my soul at
the feet of another. In the assured soul it
is kingly prodigality ; in one which cannot
forbear, it is babyhood.'"

He repeated the word "kingly" with a
musing circumflex, as if another woman would
have used a different gender, and added—

"But she would need be certain of her
lover as well as herself—which Bettine could
not be. There is something, too, in the lover.
Margaret never met Goethe.

"We all had to regret a single trait in
Margaret. Dr. Channing characteristically
referred to it once when she was a guest in
his own house, somewhat in this wise—

"' Miss Fuller, when I consider that you
are and have all that Miss —— has so long
wished for, and that you scorn her, and that
she still admires you, I think her place in
heaven will be very high.'

"Margaret," Mr. Emerson concluded,
"was a strange woman. Her eyes in some
moods were visible at night, and her hair

apparently lightened and darkened. She had unconscious clairvoyant instincts, and could read the fortune in the human face. She was most inspired when in pain. What she wrote me is expressive of her deepest nature—

"'With the intellect I always have, always shall, overcome; but that is not the half of the work. The life, the life! Oh, my God! shall the life never be sweet?'"

The flame was in the heart of this dazzling woman. If Emerson was the brain of the Concord circle, Margaret Fuller was its blood.

Of this group—the most conspicuous in its domain that has ever existed in America —Mr. Emerson was easily chief. And during his strongest years, perhaps he was more. There was something "catching" about him. No one could exactly explain or even understand it, but every one was sensible of it; so that his friends in England and America felt called upon to warn admirers that they must be on their guard, and if they sought a familiarity closer than his pocket edition, not be carried too far, for he could not encourage an imitator. Amusing stories have been told of characteristic exaggerations resulting from too much Emerson in the neighbourhood. In-

deed, one had to be more than human
to remain in the presence of a nature so
orgasmic and not betray the fact. He was
not a man to be approached closely, nor
was it well to be loved by him too dearly.
Thoreau felt the perilous singling until his
mode of speaking and tones caught the trick
of Emerson's so nearly that the two men
could hardly be separated in conversation.
What wonder that Channing, Bartol, Alcott,
and the rest, strong and stately men—more
than that, among the heavenliest bodies our
material New World has seen—felt to some
slight deflection of their orbit the unintentional, if not unconscious attraction of the
mild Jupiter so near them ! Hawthorne and
Margaret Fuller fled and saved themselves ;
but even they betrayed during their Concord
residence a faint Emersonian adumbration.
The fact is, no one meeting Emerson was
ever the same again. His natural force was
so resistless and so imperceptible that it
commanded men before they were aware.
Leaders, scholars of high cultivation, theorists,
and men of thought *de vieille roche*, who visited
the lonely eminence where he dwelt apart,
noticed the contagion. Then there were
others, a curious throng, themselves often

curiosities, who came. Concord contained
during Emerson's solstitial years a great
light-house, shining far and wide, and showing
many ships their goal, but covered with the
shreds of wrecked barques and birds of all
imaginable shapes—and some unimaginable
—which had been attracted by its clear, cold,
solitary flame. How many, just saved from
the fire, but the wax of their wings for ever
melted, went hopping about the country with
a bit of Emerson in their mouths, dissemi-
nating ordinariness and indistinctness, offer-
ing the *mime* for the Miracle Play !

But of Thoreau, that hypethral man, I
cannot say enough. Of no one did Mr.
Emerson talk so often and tenderly. The
relation adverted to between the two needs
a clearer understanding. Emerson made
Thoreau ; he was the child of Emerson,
as if of his own flesh and blood. The elder
took the younger fresh from college (rather
drowsy ; and he dozed after his return, the
Concord country was his college). Emerson
woke him, gave him his start, and immediately and astonishingly nourished him.
He lived much at Emerson's house, kept the
garden * and the home while their master

* Mr. Emerson was a man of meditation for whom

was absent in Europe, and instructed him in the mysteries of grafting and parsley.

Emerson called him "My Spartan-Buddhist, Henry," "My Henry Thoreau." With no one was he so intimate, until the disciple became as his master, adopting his accent and form, realizing his attractions and antipathies, and knowing his good and evil. The development of this sturdy bud into its sturdier flower was a perpetual delight to the philosopher. In Thoreau, he lived himself over again. He said he liked Thoreau because "he had the courage of his convictions," but I think he meant his own convictions.* In both we mark the same features: as a severe and *outre* way of looking at events, and a searching for lessons in them; avoidance of association; determination toward the expression of their ideals in their life; choice of straitened ways over broad ones,

action was too severe; and his success at garden tending is suggested by the expostulation of his son, who, alarmed at certain gestures with the spade, cautioned as follows: "Look out, papa! you'll dig your leg."

* "I told H. T. that his freedom was in the form, but he does not disclose new matter. I am familiar with all his thoughts; they are mine, quite originally dressed" (Cabot).

and refusal to turn aside for livings, rewards,
and comforts; jealousy of domestic and local
intellectual restraints, even to discontent
with the pressure of the average public sentiment; intolerance of make-shifts; keeping
away from court rooms, newspapers, and
presidents' *messages;* "reading, not the *Times*,
but the Eternities," as one said; "Standing
every man alone on his own peak," as the
other said. But the similarity does not go
much beyond these limitations. Though
Emerson was larger, Thoreau was the more
concentrated and sinewy of the two; and,
once beginning to carry out the parent's
discipline and thought into his own life, he
was uncompromising; and the end was not
seen, nor to be anticipated. He ceased to
be illustrator and personifier, or in any sense
derived. His movements, which had been
projectile, a recognition of the elder's
thorough and wholesome methods, now went
far beyond them; and, thenceforward, this
resolute man advanced his own kinetic
principles, and went his own way to his own
life. As of himself he said—

"But after manned him for *his own* stronghold."

And, thereafter, though dwelling in Concord, he lived in a far country, and was differentiated to almost a distinct species.

The variations began soon, and his loyalty plunged him occasionally into dramatic situations. I shall never forget with what gusto Mr. Emerson related to me the story of Thoreau's constancy to his political resolutions created by John Brown's execution, and his amusing week of incarceration :—

" He was served with the writ of arrest on his way to the shoe-shop; but he kept on, his shoe in his pail, to have them both mended."

" Henry was," continued Mr. Emerson, " homely in appearance, a rugged stone hewn from the cliff. I believe it is accorded to all men to be moderately homely; but he surpassed sex. He had a beautiful smile and an earnest look. His character reminds me of Massillon. One could jeopard anything on him. A limpid man, a realist with caustic eyes that looked through all words and shows and bearing with terrible perception ! He was a greater Stoic than Zeno or Scævola or Xenophanes—greater, because nothing of impurity clung to him, a man whose core and whose breath was conscience ; and not one of those giants, not one of

Europe's best, not Pitt or Burke or Grattan,
but could come to him and say, *Peccavi.*
His fault was that he brought nothing near
to his heart ; he kept all influences toward
his extremities.   Exaggerated moods we all
have to suppress ; for some amiability, or
at least reciprocity, are necessary to make
society possible.   But he thought and said
that society is always diseased, and the best
most so.   Men of note would come to talk
with him.

" ' I don't know,' he would say ; ' perhaps
a minute would be enough for both of us.'

" ' But I come to walk with you when you
take your exercise.'

" ' Ah, walking—that is my holy time.'

" And yet he was not a grave or austere
man.   I remember he made us all laugh
with his accounts of what he sometimes saw
in his walks.   What was that he told me of
the young Irishman whom he found kneeling
before his mother in the attitude of prayer ?
But, drawing nearer, he discovered that the
posture of the worshipper was merely in
order that his mother might remove a dust
particle from his eye with her tongue !

" His energy was exhausted in projecting a
new path.   He could not follow an old one,

even when it was better for him. He believed things are lies because words are.

"He was an out of doors man. He would stand in the snow for hours measuring the increments in the growth of trees. These and other similar excesses brought on an affection of the throat which caused his end. He suffered with a stoicism beyond the race, and died in great pain, nobly, refusing opiates, yielding himself to death during ' sleepless nights and days.

"His ideas of living have been condemned, but let us remember he lived them out. A Mr. Cholmondeley,* an English gentleman and graduate of Oxford, boarded while here with his mother ; and, becoming much attached to him, wished him to accompany himself to the mountains of the Yellowstone, and afterwards to South America, engaging to defray all expenses. But not only to

* Some indication as to the antecedents of this gentleman may be gleaned from the following extracts from Horace Walpole's correspondence :—

" My nephew, Lord Cholmondeley, the banker *à la mode*, has been demolished " (Horace Walpole to the Earl of Stafford, August 5, 1771).

" I am very sensible of your lordship's kindness to my nephew, Mr. Cholmondeley " (The same to the same, October 3, 1788).

those invitations, but also to another of a
trip across the States, Thoreau returned the
unvarying response—

"'I think I had better stay in Concord.'

"On one of these occasions, Cholmondeley
enlarged fancifully upon the Hamadryads
that would be found lurking among the
Druidical forests about New Orleans, and
the gorgeousness of the flora they would find
on the Amazon River, mentioning particularly
the Victoria Regia.

"'And I am expecting to find some day
the Victoria Regia on Concord River,' he
said."

The Victoria Regia for every man, he
may have meant, is to be found in the duty
at his own doorway—a habit of thought
characteristically Emerson's.*

"He refused on graduating from Harvard
to take his degree; 'It isn't worth five
dollars, he said.

* When in Naples (the first time) he wrote in his
diary longing for

"the fogs
Of close, low pine-woods in a river town;"

and he informed his brother from Paris that his own
study was the place for him; and there was always
more of fine society in his own little town than he
could command.

" I have always thought that he did not do justice to the influence of his college in forming him.

" Though living in civilization, he was the keenest observer of external nature I have ever seen. He had the trained sense of the Indian, eyes that saw in the night, his own way of threading the woods and fields, so that he felt his path through them in the densest night, without delay or interruption. He would hear a partridge fly into a bush in the dark of dawn, and guide you to the spot after day unerringly. The tread and trail of wild creatures were apparent to him by sight, hearing, and, I believe, smell; for he said that the mud-turtle obtained its peculiar odour after spring has come, *like other flowers.*"

Turtles were an object of contemplation to Thoreau. Of them he wrote :—

" I am affected by the thought that the earth nurses their eggs. They are planted in the earth, and the earth takes care of them; she is genial to them, and does not kill them. This mother is not merely inanimate and inorganic. Though the immediate mother turtle abandons her offspring, the earth and sun are kind to them. The

old turtle on which the earth rests takes
care of them, while the other waddles off."

"He was wont to assert that even in the
oldest woods one could see foreign phenomena, if always on the watch with direct
eyes and the right perception. And so he
insisted that he found revolutionary army cans
and the red Polar snow near the ponds of
Fair Haven; and the *Labrador Ledium*,
Kalmia Glauca, Canadian Lynx, a stormy
petrel, and the little auk with the tanager,
in the meadow of Sudbury. Perhaps he
idealized his vision, for he confessed :—

"'There is no power to see in the eye
itself, any more than in any other jelly; we
cannot see anything till we are possessed
with the idea of it. First, the idea or the
image of the plant occupies my thoughts, and
at length I surely see it, though it may seem
as foreign to this locality as Hudson's Bay
is.'"

As confirming Mr. Emerson's impression,
I might quote from Thoreau himself:—

"Fair Haven pond, seen from the cliffs in
the moonlight, is a sheeny lake, apparently a
boundless primitive forest, untrodden by
man; the windy surf sounding freshly and
wildly in the single pine behind you, the

silence of hushed wolves in the wilderness,
and, as you fancy, moose looking off from
the shores of the lake ; the stars of poetry
and history and unexplored nature looking
down on the scene. This light and this
hour take the civilization all out of the landscape."

" He was especially happy in forecasting
spring. He noted earliest of all the dis-
appearance of that lover of winter, the
prince's pine, and recognized first her young
grasses and vetches ; the coming of the
utricularia ; the bosky saxifrage ; the spirit-
like houstonia, and the mayflower epigæa,
pride of Plymouth hermits ; the red berries
of the trailing arbutus ; the purplish-white
flowers of the *Mikania scandens* and poly-
gonum, biding by stream-sides. He heard
first the hyla in the march, the swamp-frog
and veery. Some years he was fortunate
enough to detect in the morning twilights a
peculiar roseate tongue or halo, the snood
of Spring herself, and even her outline
in the peculiar light of the moon as re-
flected from the higher hills and mountains.
He always felt (insensible to us) the coming
heat fluent between the earth-crust and
branches.

"The fibre of nature was all through his joints and marrow, and through life he wore her livery. I don't know how long ago, far away in his ancestry (he said he was descended from the Northman, Thorer the dog-footed), she planned him, measured him for his suit.

" He will be blamed for his shortcomings in natural science, of which he made a profession; but his early death should be remembered.

" He understood the flora and the birds, but not the rocks. Out of doors he used instead of a gun a spy-glass. 'A gun,' he said, 'gives you the body, not the bird.' He would trace a fish-hawk to her nest; and then, examining the *débris* at the bottom, he would find out more about the nature of the fish-hawk than the veriest sportsman of them all. He was a naturalist, but also a poet, and would have penetrated from all external aspects of nature to the secrets of her heart. She always gave him a quick home and shelter—always just the tree at hand, with its low sloping branches ready for the poles and roof, and the boughs and foliage of spruce for a bed on which to cast his blanket. No sweeter sleeps than those ! He saturated himself with the growing wheat until he came himself to be a bearded blade.

"His out of doors life made him sensitive within doors, so that he could endure the atmosphere of few houses. He used to say, by night every dwelling gives out bad air like a slaughter-house.

"Things happened to him, came to him as they will to lovers of the woods and fields.

"I remember once a friend accosted him while they were walking with a request for an arrow-head, if he should ever find one, lamenting how fruitlessly he had searched for one.

"'They *are* rare,' said Thoreau, stooping and picking up a fragment of earth-covered substance he saw in the sod; 'and now that you have an opportunity, you had better examine this!' And he presented a fine specimen from which he finished disengaging the earth-rust. An accident? I do not know. Sometimes I have thought the entire woods were a *cache* for him; he had such secrets of hiding things and finding them again. His invention of a new lead pencil was quite characteristical. He could buy none that would suit him, so he determined to make some. After close study and ex- periment, he produced the most excellent pencil I have ever seen, and manufactured some hundreds of them, which he distributed among his friends. A few found their way to a neighbouring city, and he was approached by capitalists with liberal offers to manufacture them in quantities for commercial purposes. But he refused, with the remark that he merely wished to make a good pencil for his own use; and the secret died with him. He overflowed with ridicule for household utensils, etc., such as the store-keepers offer, and the few such things he used he provided for himself, and they were much superior and more convenient. Did he want a portmanteau or box? Forthwith he produced it, stripping the bark off a tree, joining by dovetail without tack or nail, and chamfering the edges and bottom.

"He was a close student of a few books. He liked the ethnic scriptures. Cholmondeley had given him some rare and costly copies of the Bhagavad-Gita and other bibles. His style has been sometimes criticized as opaque, but that is a quality frequently found in the reader. It was a style that refused compromise as did the man. 'If the spirit of poetry,' he said, 'chooses to descend upon me as I stand still, it is well; if not, I will not go in search of her. Here, on this rugged

soil of Massachusetts, I take my stand,
baring my brow to the breeze of my own
country and invoking the genius of my own
words.'

"It is better to translate him than Epictetus
or Marcus Antoninus. He looked inward,
inward at the soul of things. Conscientious,
earnest, he talked in plain words to the
superstitious, and commanded his publishers
not to change a line. Thus his pages seem
profane and sometimes blasphemous. He
did not hesitate at shocking any weather-
worn creed or belief. Men called him
sceptic; but he was too conscientious to go
to church. It was curious how much his
opinion was sought, considering how much
it was derided. No sooner did any extraordinary news arrive than every one must
know what Thoreau thought about the last
happening. His poetry is of a new order.
The poem on Smoke is instinct with the
spirit of Simonides :—

'Light-winged Smoke ! Icarian bird,
Melting thy pinions in thy upward flight ;
Lark without song, and messenger of dawn,
Circling above the hamlets as thy nest ;
Or else, departing dream and shadowy form
Of midnight vision, gathering up thy skirts ;

By night star-veiling, and by day
Darkening the light, and blotting out the sun,
Go thou, my incense, upward from this hearth,
And ask the gods to pardon this clear flame.'

" He was penetrated with the elder classical influence ; he breathed the antique. Yet it was impossible for him to copy words or anything.

" There was during his literary life between himself and Mr. Ticknor an inequality of temperament and taste, by which the publishing house of that gentleman was always prevented from doing Thoreau justice. Consequently, the *Atlantic* has published for Thoreau, but not his best work. Mr. Greeley was his most influential publishing friend. Thoreau has an always increasing number of readers, and the selectest class of any American in all Christendom. The 'Week on the Concord River' is his noblest work, pervaded with delightful ideas. And you must have the 'Letters and Select Poems' of his I have lately edited. I will give them to you.

" He had a great contempt for those who made no effort to gauge accurately their own powers and weaknesses, and by no means spared himself, of whom he said that a man gathers materials to erect a palace, and finally concludes to build a shantee with them.

"'You have heard from a great many,' he wrote to a friend in Springfield. 'How long since you had a letter from yourself?'

"'You pay yourself for your riches,' he wrote again; 'what becomes of *you?*'"

Others of Thoreau's *bon mots*, approved by Mr. Emerson, I treasured :—

"Occasion wears front hair."

"A poor man's cow, a rich man's child dies."

"Sleep is half a dinner."

"Good heart, weak head." *(This is Thoreau-ish.)*

"What men do, not what they promise."

"People are less careful to avoid evil than its appearance."

"No animal is so patient as the fretful porcupine."

"Let the muse lead the muse. If the muse accompany, she is no muse, but an amusement."

"It is the art of mankind to polish the world, and every one who works is scrubbing in some part."

"Could there be an accident so sad as to be respected for something better than we are?"

" If we made the true distinction, we should almost all of us be seen to be in the alms-house for souls."

"Who is most dead—a hero by whose monument you stand, or his descendants of whom you never heard?"

"The farmer is an enchanted labourer."

"Never, except in the case of women and children, act on the supposition that people's regard for you can be higher than yours for them."

"Sometimes we are inclined to class those who are once-and-a-half witted with the half-witted, because we appreciate only a third of their wit."

And from Saadi :—

" Keep the door to your mouth shut, and I cannot tell whether you deal in jewels or small ware."

" The cat is a tiger to the mouse, but is herself a mouse to the tiger."

"When you determine to fight, be sure that you are stronger than your adversary, or that you have a swifter pair of heels."

" Of a truth every one is born with a tendency to Islamism, and it is owing to his parents his becoming a Jew, a Christian, or a Majoosie."

"To the nymphs of paradise purgatory would be hell, and ask the inhabitants of hell whether purgatory is not paradise."

" O Lord of the World ! Those who are Zâhids will not accept of money; and they who have money are not Zâhids."

Emerson quoted not seldom as from Thoreau the figure—

> "When Autumn bleeds
> In all the maples ; "

and said the following from Ennius was often on Thoreau's lips—

> " *Ego deum genus dici et dicam cœlitum,*
> *Sed eos non curare, opinor, quid agat humanum*
> *genus ;*
> *Nam, si curent, bene bonis sit, male malis quod nunc*
> *abest.*"

And this from Shelley—

> " The day that dawns in fire will die in storms,
> Even though the noon be calm."

It was Thoreau's theory that the universe grows by destruction of itself. The process of development from the nebulous completes its decay.

> " And thefts from satellites and rings
> And broken stars I drew ;
> And out of spent and aged things
> I framed the world anew."

His belief is epitomized in Pindar's eighth Olympic—

> " A man doing fit things
> Forgets Hades."

Nec quid hymen quid amor quid sint connubia curat.

The barque foundered too early, but surely it sails another sea ?

It was not easy for human nature to honour one who honoured not it, and so he lived in antagonism outward or inward with most of those he met. He was a forsaken traveller on a solitary roadway through the land of Noman, and few there be that find it. Emerson referred to him the words—

" I can see no one who is able to fill the place he has left here, no causes at work to produce one who even has a tendency to fill it."

To Parker Pillsbury, who approached him on the subject of religion the winter before his death, he replied gently, " One world at a time."

It was a grim day that he was borne from the village meeting-house to his grave near Hawthorne in Sleepy Hollow. Only a little company of friends were present. Mr.

Emerson spoke a few words after the coffin was lowered.

As Thoreau exhibited Emerson the recluse, so Amos Bronson Alcott, a most benign, saintly, and unworldly man when I knew him, was a joyous and buoyant embodiment of Mr. Emerson socially. For Emerson was not what one would term "talkative;" indeed, it is seldom one meets a man more held in duress by his own thought. When he was surprised into utterance it was mostly a monologue of oral reflections which seemed to be addressed to a widely read and thoughtful audience, and which always exacted much of the listener. It is somewhat remarkable that a man who has given more movement to thought than almost any other since Plato, should have shown in habit so little sympathy with this law by which men most naturally receive ideas ! But I think he secretly found the simplest conditions under which people meet irksome.

" Parties of pleasure, yes, parties of *ennui,*" he once remarked. And again, " When one meets his mate, society begins ; " expressions of a man who, although among us, is not of us.

And yet I recall no words about conversa-

tion better than his. He apprehended it
rightly; he called it, "A series of intoxications;" "The right metaphysical professor;"
"The true school of philosophy;" and said,
"We must be warmed by the fire of sympathy,
and be brought into the right conditions and
angles of vision."

"When you answer," it was his maxim,
"address the meaning, not the words." And
his tenth beatitude was, "Blessed is he who
giveth the answer that cannot be answered."

But he did not commonly exemplify this.
The conspicuous illustration of it was Mr.
Alcott, who had a much more extended
adaptiveness. To him the meeting of human
beings in converse was what the communion-
table is to Christians. He founded the
drawing-room conversation as a means of
culture, a more valuable gift than Emerson's
of the Lyceum. Its method, by which a
leader discourses upon some theme at leisure,
answering questions which are farther discussed in the freedom of informal exchange,
is more natural and probably more rewarding
than either lecturing or preaching, especially
among people where similar conditions of
receptivity prevail. Mr. Alcott's field was
limited, because his philosophy was not often

vascular, so that, as Fichte said of himself, he could only succeed with "brave good people." But who that met him in the *conversazioni* which he made so popular can forget the experience—the master's "solar face," framed in that wealth of hair in which the white breath of his soul had been caught and kept; his pleasant fervours; his irresistible hyperboles; his colours, dilatations, magniloquence, glorious soarings to the great might have been; sublime and ideal chimeras; the winning wilfulness with which he presented a sometimes erroneous philosophy; his pictures, delicate rather than distinct, and somewhat bleached, as if conceived amid etiolated conditions; his fugitive answerings, orphic, subtle, like quicksilver, and, even when merely amœbæan, the participants having dropped out, and the ground beneath sounding hollow to every ear but his, so surpassingly complete and master-like, always satisfying the questioner, who enjoyed if he could not acquiesce.

Though often philodoxical rather than philosophical, he was always in sympathy with the highest motives that can elevate the human soul, and received from God the gift of lofty inspirations, singularly incommensur-

H

able, from which Emerson with others grate-
fully drank.   His sacred enthusiasms, which
penetrated his hearers as if they had drunken
sunbeams, buoyed his step to the last, sounded
in his voice like an angelus, and dwelt in his
eyes long after they had lost their speech and
feeling, and became otherwise rayless like a
vault.   He had a soul of candour ; whatever
other expression his face wore, that never left
it, and his smile had such faith that it made
melancholy a sin.   He cherished a sweet
sense of the loyalty of friendship, and believed devoutly in the Concord saviours.   No
one circulated with more enthusiastic per-
versity west and east, with now and then a
conscientious obolus from Emerson, the coin
of mutual gratulation, acceptable possibly to
numismatists, but hardly current on Olympus.
He possessed before groups a manner
never for a moment fatiguing.   He knew the
secret of teaching by talk, and his demeanour
at gatherings was always illuminated by a
gentle politeness and interpretation of others.

He understood how to open the eyes of
people without contradicting them.   Children
especially were susceptible to the charm.
What Landor makes the Greek child, Ternissa,
say of Epicurus, reminds me closely of what

the child of an acquaintance said of Mr.
Alcott :—

" I love to hear him talk. He is so plain,
and tells me so much I didn't know, fastening
it on to what I did know; and he has so
much patience, and looks so kindly, as if he
were waiting for more questions."

Of Mr. Alcott Emerson said—

"Bronson Alcott is a man supremely self-
conscious. Socrates thought Athens ought
to support him; and Alcott thinks Boston
Commonwealth ought to support *him*—and
it ought! His life is full of beatitudes.
Wordsworth should have come to him for the
origin of the Pedlar. He has no regard for
wealth. Once an admirer sent him a twenty-
dollar gold piece from Boston. About a
week after, a mendicant, passing his door,
asked alms.

" ' I have nothing,' said Alcott, answering
from habit—' or yes, stay ; I have, too ; wait
a minute ! '

"And, running into his house, he returned
with the gold coin, which he handed to the
beggar. He took it and vanished. I believe a week or so afterwards he returned it
to Mr. Alcott, with the remark that he found
he was not able to either keep or spend it.

"Alcott is the best reader of Plato living. He talks exquisitely. A reporter offered, good-naturedly, to report his conversations, but he failed to reproduce the delicate inflections and tints of thought which form their charm. He has a passion for writing, but he cannot write, he has no gift that way. His pages are anchylozed. I always feel sad when he brings anything to read to me. He used to say that Jesus was intensely feminine; always spiritually apprehensive and respondent to the thought rather than its expression.

"His ways of teaching were new and un-popular. He was exposed to persecution on account of them. But they are sure to be adopted, because they are based on human nature.

"He came to Concord from Germantown, Pa., about forty years ago. The name of the family was Alcox. He changed it to Alcott. His wife was from one of the most excellent families in Boston. There will never be enough credit given to that woman for what he and his daughters have done.

"Louisa was born about thirty-four years after her father, and on the same day. She is a natural source of stories. When she was seven years old she was the delight of the com-

munity, writing dramas and building theatres
at her father's and the neighbours' houses.
She composed a hymn while yet a girl; wrote
a book (which has been printed under the
name of 'Moods') when she was sixteen;
another, a book of fables, before she was
twenty. At nineteen the papers began buy-
ing her stories. She did not want to grow to
womanhood. She went out as a governess,
and wrote a story of her experiences for the
Atlantic; but they could not understand it,
and told her she had better continue as a
teacher.

"She never was sick until she went into the
army as nurse, and has never been well since.
She took a trip to Europe, which was an un-
doubted benefit. She produced her hospital
sketches in 1865, and is now (1868), I believe, bringing out what will be her best yet,
'Little Women.' We all think this is due to
her publishing friend, who told her she must
write a girl's book, while she insisted she
could not. It is often the case that publishers
understand authors better than they do themselves. She is, and is to be, the poet of
children. She knows their angels.

"May won Ruskin's praise for her wonderful copies of Turner, which were sold at great

profit. But Mr. Alcott respected Louisa's genius because it was original. May's pleasant room at home was much admired by our Concord folk. She had Thoreau's genius with materials. The cover of the walls and floor, the finish and adornment of the furniture, were the work of her own hands. The mirror formed the farthest, inner centre of successive frames of different woods, so that in it one's face was like a picture in perspective, 'reached by courteous approaches,' as her father said."

Of Transcendentalism, Mr. Alcott remarked, "It means that there is more in the mind than enters it through the senses."

He was a great believer in heredity. When the children did wrong, he said—

"It is the fault of the old folks. What we are is the result of our ancestors. Choice," he insisted, "implies apostacy. The pure, unsullied soul is above choice."

And again, "Those who learn by heart are taught from the heart, a spontaneous teacher."

His conscientiousness, like Thoreau's, brought him once to the inside of a jail, from which he was released by Mr. Hoar.

· He was a living rebuke to gross animal

feeding. Like all Pythagoreans, he was not an eater of flesh.

Is it he or Mr. Emerson Charles Kingsley called "Cousin Cramchild"? It would have been neither if Mr. Kingsley had known of whom he was speaking. Mr. Alcott's "St. John the Evangelist" is an utterance wholly after the heart of the great Englishman.

TRANSCENDENTALISM.

TRANSCENDENTALISM.

"THE Puritans came here," said Mr. Emerson one day, "in a revolt against forms. Why should they have kept any, then? Why accept baptism and the bread and wine of the Supper, and refuse the foot-washing, which was at least as strongly emphasized? They were right, nobly; but they stopped short. Is *any* form necessary? Do we need any gift or foreign force? Can we not be self-sustaining? See this divinity of daisies around us. Can we not be level to them? What need is there of miracles? That Jesus lived purely was his strong argument.

" Virgil said to Dante—

> " 'Let us not talk of these things ;
> Let us look and pass on.'

"But there must be an effort to merge religion into literature, and realize theology; for man's highest good is concerned. The elimination of scholasticism and subtleties

would be healthful ; and divine lives would
the more hasten to become common."

He paused a moment, and I felt encouraged to ask—

"What is Transcendentalism, Mr. Emerson ?"

He was silent, and then said, with a
humorous emphasis—

"Well, why do you ask *me?* It isn't, I
suppose, a commodity or 'Plan of Salva-
tion,' or anything concrete ; not, surely, an
'established church ;' rather, unestablished ;
not even bread, perhaps, but a leaven
hidden." *(Here is the answer.)*

He continued more seriously—

"If we will only see that which is about
us, we shall see also above. Is God far from
any of us ? There is an equality of the
human spirit to the world's phenomena. We
look neither up to the universe nor down to
it, but confront it, And the soul should
always bear itself thus in the presence of the
natural objects which suggest and express
God, are His revelations.

"The Transcendentalist sees everything
as Idealist. That is, all events, objects, etc.,
seen, are images to the consciousness. It
is the thought of them only one sees. You

shall find God in the unchanged essence of
the universe, the air, the river, the leaf;
and in the subjective unfolding of your
nature, the determination of the private
spirit, everything of religion. As for the
name, no one knows who first applied the
name."

Once he mentioned Kant; and the Critik
of Pure Reason was, perhaps, a remote an-
cestor of Transcendentalism. I could not
receive then the full content of Mr. Emerson's words on Idealism. Now, with the
commentaries of the years, they are plain;
but it is not necessary to present the subject
here, it having become familiar. The impression of Transcendantalism which his speech
conveyed was that he esteemed it less as a
gospel or even revelation than as a rebuke of
the temper which accepts mediators, incarna-
tions, and go-betweens; a protest, appeal,
aspiration for direct relations between God
and man, unencroached upon by any " word."
The Bible is a sacred book of all nations, of
value as the record of a religion. The book
of nature (by which is intended all objects
that have retained simplicity) is the "word
of God." The Kingdom of Heaven certainly
comes with observation. As all material

forms necessarily lived before in Him, so we
find Him in them now.

Literally, a passing beyond all media in
the approach to the Deity, Transcendentalism
contained an effort to establish, mainly by a
discipline of the intuitive faculty, direct intercourse between the soul and God. "I am
the door," said Jesus; "no one cometh unto
the Father but by me." "Yet," pleaded the
new Evangel, "are we not brothers? Let
us come as thou camest, to thy Father and
to our Father."

It is often the fate of a new doctrine to be
carried farther than its founder intended.
That the conservatives hastened to demand
the establishment of a chair of Apologetics in
the viewless Theological Seminary of Concord was natural enough; but the surprise of
the philosopher and his friends was awakened
by the eccentricities of sundry fanatics whose
heads had been hurt by Apollo's quoits
thrown wild. They announced theories, as
they said, beyond Emerson, and yet called
them his; they even deified him as a being
of mist and fire far in advance, and leading
in the path. Though he did not deny that
he could not make it straight, how straight
were those of the accepted faith-bringers?

And so they clambered their Emersonian trail
up the mountain until it disappeared among
atmospheres that would not support spiritual
life. There was much heroic even in these
eccentrics. What though their inspiration
of rarified air did create some excesses, before
which it is an effort to keep the countenance ;
and the sacred fire of their fane proved to be
a spurious phlogiston, causing inflammation
rather than flame,—it is to be remembered
that these were brave men who stood for
something; men not "to be killed among
the bats as a bird, among the birds as a
bat ; " and a heart unstirred by their devotion
is cold indeed.

But the glory of the sunrise was in the eyes
of those already in the immediate religious
and intellectual neighbourhood; and the
number included some of the purest men
and profoundest thinkers in the country.
They cared less for the name than for the
ideas clustered around it. To them it was
enough that the faith vindicated the freedom
of the soul against all forms of fatalism, and
pronounced man a being of eternity instead
of a worm of the dust. From such a faith
they would drink as from a stream of cold
refreshment, and be satisfied without inquiry

as to whether it flowed from or toward the
mountain of Omniscience. What other
doctrine said so many true words by the
way? and so no matter whither the way
led.

Their first concrete expression was the
Dial. To turn the pages within its faded
old lilac covers now is to bring again the
atmosphere of those creative days, their
nobility and their heroisms. Margaret Fuller
was the first editor, and although her
catholicity, too large to permit a waste-
basket, admitted uninspired witnesses to the
uselessness of Saviours and discussions of
the universality of the Holy Spirit in a
soprano key, yet so high was the motive and
so strenuous the impulse of its founders, that
every number contained expressions in-
valuable and quite equivalent to the propaga-
tion of themselves, despite stupidities and
delusions. Mr. Emerson did manfully his
share, assuming the editorship, but finally
relinquishing a work so unnatural to him.
William Ellery Channing was perhaps its
most delightful writer, with such opulent com-
panions as Theodore Parker, J. Freeman
Clarke, C. A. Dana, James Russell Lowell,
Frederic Hedge, C. A. Bartol, J. C. Cabot,

C. P. Cranch, and others. The *Dial* was
a horologe of the dawn, and should have
marked the hours longer.

All this was fifty years ago ; and the *Dial's*
shadow now is only seen in Alcott's garden.
One can hardly wander of an afternoon after
summer is flown, here where the Concord
School of Philosophy holds its intellectual
festivals, in the presence of statuettes of
Plato, Emerson, Harris, Howison, Thoreau,
Voltaire, Pestalozzi, Mulford, Dr. Jones, and
others which haunt the arbours and grace
the walks of the parterres and grove of apple-
trees, even to Hillside Chapel, where Webster's Dictionary is the only book in sight,
without feeling that he is in a hygienic atmosphere, friendly to a larger and sane liberty of
religious meditation.

There are those who believe that the ghost
of Transcendentalism will rise again, and are
even waiting to see the stone rolled away
from its sepulchre ; but may we not accept
this emancipation as inheritance, as all that
will come out from it for the healing of the
nations ?

Did he from whose loins it was drawn expect more, a present faith ?

I think not. As he desired to construct

I

no system of theology or moral science,
never giving us a system nor completing his
" Natural History of the Spirit or Intellect "
(sometimes called one and sometimes the
other), so his Transcendentalism is to be
regarded as a fragment, existing less as a
religious idiosyncracy, much less a passing
fashion, than as a lifting and permanent
force in general religious culture. As a
modifying influence in thought, as an impulse toward a finer life, it became a power.
Its subtle suggestions, its aspirations; that
which it stood for and symbolized ; its
exultant, soaring spirit—these gave it meaning to every elevated soul drawn into it.
Where it touched the practical duties of life,
its touch was recognized as honest. The
promises it made to the believer never insult
the purity of religious motive, and resemble,
so far as literal fulfilment is concerned, those
made by Jehovah to the fathers. As to the intuitions as a conduit of the spirit or over-soul,
Mr. Emerson had never a doubt. He trusted
his completely, and even gave them a
feminine credence in his relations with persons. If he had any superstition it was this.
In a quaker-talk he said—

" I do not pretend to any commandment

or large revelation. But if at any time I form a plan, propose a journey or a course of conduct, I find, perhaps, a silent obstacle in my mind that I cannot account for. Very well; I let it lie, think it may pass away; if it does not pass away, I yield to it, obey it. You ask me to describe it. I cannot describe it. It is not an oracle, not an angel, not a dream, not a law; it is too simple to be described; it is but a grain of mustard-seed. But such as it is, it is something which the contradiction of all mankind could not shake."

He was a pilgrim of the invisible, and, both by heritage and growth, without the capacity of sin. Transcendentalism to him was, to be faithful to the revelations that come to the soul, and are recognized by it as true.

Once in later years, and in his own study, I ventured to ask him—

"Mr. Emerson, what of personal immortality?"

He turned gently some pages, and handed me one which read somewhat as follows :—

"The youth puts off the illusions of the child. The man puts off the ignorance and tumultuous fancies of youth; proceeding thence, puts off the egotism of manhood, and

becomes at last a public and universal soul,
hence rising to great heights, but also rising
to realities, until the last garment of egotism
falls and he is with God, shares the will and
immensity of the first cause."

I received this immediately as a declaration of belief in the final absorption of all
individualities into an original and active
entity which is continually creative. And
perhaps this is a form of immortality familiar
to his meditation. But afterwards I thought
I saw in the statement not necessarily a projection of his own faith, but (such was his
habit of answering habits and moods of
thought rather than forms of expression) a
mild censure of the question itself, as if, indeed, he had replied : Do not question ; for
character and destiny are the same, and ex-
cessive canvassing about being prolonged betrays a weakness of self-conceit which destroys the possibility. To such an attitude
the answer must be that the teleology of life,
so far as we can follow it, is that of the type,
not the individual.

For at another time he wrote, and the
passage was inspired—

"I have a house, a closet which holds my
books, a stable, a garden, a field ; are these,

any or all, a reason for refusing the angel who beckons me away, as if there were no room or skylight elsewhere that could reproduce for me as my wants require?"

He spoke of God varyingly; sometimes almost personally as if synonymous with perfect manliness, again as an immanent spirit, often as a pervasive force, *It.* He held faith rigidly to fact, so far as we can see fact. "It is not permitted," he said to me, "to believe in opposition to the guidepost. We can only remember that it does not travel the road it points out. We can travel it, but that road, no other!"* In order to appreciate Mr. Emerson's newness and revolution, it is necessary to read the literature of his day, for his doctrines are common property now.

His evangel was faith in man and man's final victory. The future was serene. Almost the last words I was ever to hear him utter were with a smile and cheer regarding a doubt he could not dispel.

* So Carlyle: "A course wherein clear faith cannot go with you may be worse than none; if clear faith go never so slightly against it, then it *is* certainly worse than none" (Carlyle, letter to Emerson, February 3, 1835).

"For that," he said, "we must wait until to-morrow morning." By

> "That great and grave transition
> Which may not king or priest or conqueror spare,
>   And yet a babe can bear."

The morrow's morning has come to him.

PRESENCE.

PRESENCE.

WHEN I recall Mr. Emerson personally, I
recognize that a man more impersonal one
seldom meets. There was nothing pronounced about him. Presence (in one meaning) he had none, because he was without
the consciousness, self-esteem, and self asser-
tion which go so far to constitute it. But
there was that behind the withdrawn manner
which took possession with an exclusiveness
no personal fascinations or magnetism could
equal or explain. To every comer he was
a fact and experience, undissuadable, penetrating to the region of motive and source of
volition; and from the first moment, his was
the " morning light which shines more and
more unto the perfect day."

At the time of our first meeting, Mr.
Emerson was sixty-two. His tall, slender
figure had made slight obeisance to age ; but
the earlier portraits of him I had been
familiar with ill-prepared me for his changed

expression. The aggressive physiognomy was
still there; the delicate, severe lips and
piercing eyes. But they rarely flashed now,
wearing instead an introspective grey; and
the lips were rather those of a seer than a
poet. The hair alone had kept its native
colour, like dark wine. Both Rowse's and
Wyatt Eaton's rather than Griswold's portraits
revive him faithfully as he was at this time,
and during the few later years that I saw
him. Rowse especially has reproduced the
large featuring of his face, with that wise,
determined nose (called straight, like the
Damascus road) which other Emersons have,
and the tender, shrewd eyes, that until the
very end kept so much sunshine in them.
And what eyes they were! Whatever they
looked at, they looked into, and that effort-
lessly. Such are not ordinary eyes; they are
divining rods. I have noticed that most men
successful in values, business men of the first
order, have the same inquisitive peer. Under
excitement his look was illuminated, and betrayed by turns the sagacity of the man of
affairs and the "vision" of the clairvoyant.
His more tranquil regard continually revealed
yourself to yourself like the limpidity of a
clear pool.

But the regnant feature of Mr. Emerson's personal contact was his voice : in converse agreeable, kindly, incisive, it was only to be heard when everything was congruous and still. But who that ever listened to it in public has forgotten the healthful experience ? Not resonant like Phillips', and presenting fewer contrasts with itself than Beecher's, it seemed as neither of these to carry, as some rivers carry gold, the speaker's soul in it. And the voice, like the soul, knew no falling inflections. Calm and equable, the monologist went on, the voice always raised, suspense after suspense, still inconclusive when the auditor looked for rest, the theme growing clear until the postponed emphasis of the final pause, and that still an upward pitch ; the lesson of which made me puzzle and ponder, and finally appeared to be ethical rather than rhetorical—that on all subjects we discourse inadequately, and can never come to a period. As if he should say : It is time to stop, but not to finish. There is more to be added to complete the presentation, but it cannot be spoken now on account of something else which must follow.

So he always stood on the rostrum, having cast away all the tricks that orators hold

dear, gestureless, save now and then a slight
movement of the hand, repelling as from the
cold pole of a magnet; his eyes searching
his manuscript, or raised over all of us and
gazing forward into space, sometimes in the
presence of a luminous expression, glowing
like the lenses of some great light-gatherer;
uttering sentence after sentence, with the
accent of a man who insists on this present
statement, but who believes that we cannot
here come to the whole truth of the thing,
and shall never quite find the end of it.

For the rest, so lifted and extraordinary
was the elevation from which he approached
the subjects he discussed; so clear his
medium, and removed from lower currents
and "occasions"; such was his insight,
mastery, and moderation,—that he soon
created in his audience a fine surprise, and,
without delay, his own nerve and spirit. Then,
such was his fairness and solicitation, so
liberated was the manner of his address from
dogmatism and self-assertiveness, that his
audience was fain to project him free of the
local circumstance, and to identify his presence as representative in this busy and
material age of that solitary and timeless
group of natures, the choice of all ages.

But the completed benediction was after he descended from the enforced dignity of the platform, and apart from the exacting restraints of the study. For, creator of the Lyceum though he was, it was in talk, when he *would* talk, that he was most delighting. No one of his group but Mr. Alcott rivalled him here.

Nobility characterized his deportment. Elevating is a weak word with which to describe the influence of his gentle serenity upon men; for even quite above themselves were they lifted by his presence, and found their highest moments his common ones. The cause of this was that all his thoughts and life were abreast of the Holy Spirit and tried by it, so that every phenomenon assumed its natural place, demanding attention, but at no moment throwing the soul out of its relation with the Unseen. Even in those days when he was disturbing the movement of all the intelligent forces around him, and the entire atmosphere was in commotion because of him, there was one point of absolute calm, the centre of the cyclone.

As has been with less truth said of another, and yet not entirely appropriately of him, "He was beautifully unfit to walk in the ways of other men;" not entirely appropriately, for, although solitary, he was a welcoming man, tendered a noble regard, meeting every one without shyness or stiffness, interesting himself to make the most of the occasion, so that his presence was a continual solicitation and reward. Although quiet almost to reserve (I never heard him laugh), his social bearing was distinguished by an old-school politeness, with just enough polish to divert the suspicion that his retirement had made him rustic ; and his slight, half foreign etiquette was so uplifted by the presence of the moral sense, that his manners were celestial.

His conversation was always in the low tone of one accustomed to being listened to, and presupposed a philologist's knowledge of words, so that the language was followed doubtingly at first, but soon companionably, and, anon, it was plain that he opened horizons and left on almost everything he touched a remnant of originality. Moreover, one had with him the perpetual delight of hearing a thing said in its best way. You listened now to a quaint anecdote or satire, and now to an epithet, comparison, or excerpt, touched gently or sharply with his own

criticism, until you breathed the high atmosphere where your companion dwelt, not as a
spectator but as familiar; and, after parting,
you remembered, more even than his vivid
talk, his simple ways, the home-like feeling he
diffused, and the forgetfulness that you were
in the presence of our foremost American.

He was an intent listener. One was
quite sure of his appreciation and ready
sympathy, if deserved. But there was always
in his personality a certain resistance; and
even when his companionship was most
gentle and encouraging, it was searching and
pungent like the odour and flavour of certain
flowers and herbs. His books are aromal
with the same quality.

He disliked odd people, and during his
most useful years he was compelled to meet
a great many. Sometimes it seemed as if
they would overrun him, even drawing from
him, *àpropos* of introductions, the droll demur,
"Whom God hath put asunder, why should
man join together?" But he was always
patient, and tried to free each one from his
peccant humours and triteness, and discover
what was his advantage. How often did the
peripatetic philosopher without honour in his
own land find here the right royal arch for

his Spanish castle, and the unappreciated poet wings and a farriery for his limping palfrey!

Anything that excited remark in dress and demeanour he avoided by instinct. I re-member he returned from New York, and told me that Mr. Walt Whitman, by invita-tion dining with him at the Astor House, had come without his coat! The extremes met then, though undoubtedly he enjoyed the democratic poet, despite the odour his verses perspire. Long enough after the occurrence to divert any suspicion of a con-nection, Mr. Emerson said—

"Dress should reveal the spirit. There are men so brutally wilful and indifferent to civilization that they remind one of the veldt, the dhow, and the kraal. They ought to go about, their faces smeared with woad, in skins of wild animals, with a bone-club on their shoulders and a sword of shark tooth, beating drums of fish skin."

And again—

"Manners should bespeak the man, inde-pendent of fine clothing. The general does not need a brilliant coat."

"If we could only dress as the earth does! She always looks young."

He was a most salutary companion. His very nearness was an abstersion. To him, there was but one foundation of genuine courtesy as of genuine character, and that was the moral sense, so that though he never preached against bad physical habits and morals, his presence did not permit them. The sobriety, directness, honesty, and conscientiousness which he infused into a man were antiseptic, and eliminated slovenly and unfortunate habits of mind and body.*

It was taken for granted as a basis of companionship with him that one was living in constant obedience to the demands of his highest nature. He believed that the intellect and the moral sentiment should not be separated. Crass instincts he could forgive, and he had an almost divine patience with weakness and

* Mr. Emerson said he smoked very (and we all know how he spared that overworn word) rarely, and never until he was fifty. He was a punctual man. I remember one afternoon we were going to drive. As I came into his room, prompt to the moment, I saw that he was already waiting. Every book and manuscript were put out of reach, not even the newspaper before him ; but there he sat on the edge of the lounge, his coat on his arm, his hat in his hand. I never knew him a minute late at any appointment. The example of course caught me—at a cost, I suppose, of years.

even indolence, but none with dishonesty. He anticipated the disclosures of Rémusat as he did the discoveries of Darwin, and despised the first Bonaparte because he cheated at cards.

"It is one of those acts," he said to me, "which only men of a certain kind can commit. It cannot be extenuated."

So his bearing had a certain translucency, and begat it.

"When two persons," he remarked once in my hearing, "are not happy with one another, fence and parry with one another, instead of meeting, are not all of their expressions a little impertinent ? " (out of place).

"We drop everything and arrive at simplicity, which is the perfection of manners."

Incompetence, weakness of will, vacillating motives, nay, even stupidity, might be overlooked ; but traits of hypocrisy, never. Less endurable to him than even the flippant folk who thought to entertain him with their theological cavilling, was the approach of these persons of superficial etiquette and attired manners who were too polite for good breeding, donning courtesies for the sake of experiment or occasion. But even the genuflections of these toy-shop gentry, and the deeper disease of dissimulating natures pretending to the possession of tastes and sympathies they did not own and did not care to own, he would strive to antidote, often by pointed questions which would disclose to these confecting people the real state of things, or by a severe simplicity of demeanour which afforded uneasy contrast.

" He was a friend, a more than friend, austere
To make one know one's self and make him fear.
He gave that touch too noble to be kind,
To wake to life the mind within the mind."

But when the affectations were too pronounced, his phrases grew quiet and brief; he became reticent or disappeared. A passage of Wordsworth reminds me of him :—

" Plain his garb,
Such as might suit a rustic sire, prepared
For Sabbath duties ; yet he was a man
Whom no one could have passed without remark.
Active and nervous was his gait ; his limbs
And his whole figure breathed intelligence.
Time had compressed the freshness of his cheek
Into a narrower circle of deep red,
But had not tamed his eye that, under brows
Shaggy and gray, had meanings which he brought
From years of growth—like a being made
O' many beings."
    Excursion, " The Wanderer."

But words do not touch nerves; I would
that they could, that you might find herein
himself as well as his utterances, so that this
record might be, as Mr. Walt Whitman hoped
of his "Leaves of Grass," a man and not
a book. But I forbear, failing to recall him
as I knew him—genial, mild-mannered,
breathing an enchanted youth, though already
beyond the years when men begin to think
about dying or are half dead.

A word about the nest and its good lares!
Mr. Emerson rarely spoke of himself, but
he had the passion for home which is
characteristic of all manly natures, and told
me that he believed in large families. His
mother had twelve brothers and sisters—five
sisters and one brother older than herself,
three sisters and three brothers younger—and
his father and mother had eight children.

I asked him once about his boyhood, but
the brief answer gave small glimpse of boyish
spirits and joys; and reading in the meeting-
house was probably his nearest to a boy's
sins. Perhaps he was a man who never had
a boyhood; I think it must have been always
aged. And so not least among the marvels
he awakened, was the pleasant query how one
who never was a boy himself could cherish

so subtle a sympathy with a boy's weakness and work and gladness and troubles.

But, notably from the mother, there was an atmosphere of charm and peace in the home that no jollity could substitute. All through the child life, the sweetness of living for one another was exemplified. Through youth into manhood, it was still the gentle order of the family. William taught school to help Waldo through college ; Waldo taught school to help Edward ; and Edward taught school to help Charles—all graduating from Cambridge between 1818 and 1828. Simplicity and mutual deference and love were the law of the household.

:

METHOD.

METHOD.

How exacting is aroused youth! It claims without shame every sacrifice; and, if it could, would lay its head by the face of God. Out of its twilight some path it must find or force. What grace, then, in the inimitable man to shorten for a time to half-length the arm by which his neophyte has been held, and vouchsafe as to *the what, the when,* and *the how* wise disclosures, not by didactic precept, but simply by showing his own ways; not, of course, that they could become another's, but that so best could another get his own. This last rare gift I seek in these two concluding chapters to pass on to the new generation, trying thereby to render such return as the great giver would direct. This is solely my purpose, and to abstain from all judgment and the like. Such an attitude is foreign to me when I think of him. Incomparable and beyond speech incommensurable is he; and the

greatest have been his interpreters. They
have spread the profound and conspicuous
elements of his character, and taken up and
carried on his lofty message. Their decisions
are of record familiar wherever his name is
known, and history has given him his own
place. Of so exalted a man my opinions and
encomium are of no worth; but, especially
to those young hearts to whom is this address,
my experiences have value in proportion to
their nearness—provided always that they
are given with faithfulness and frankness;
traits which should always belong to narrators.
To omit a characteristic incident or mode is
an unfortunate prejudgment. The subtract-
ing fact only injures when suppressed. It
would seem that a biographer literally takes
a life when he takes from it that which alone
unites it with other lives. A perfect hero
with either his virtues or his vices "writ in
water," is transhuman; and so valueless to
the world as an example, because it can find
no *point d'appui* in so much symmetry. I
noticed Mr. Emerson invariably made these
distinctions and expected them. No man
ever lived who has less to lose by their
observance. Strangers who sought him for
the first time, and found his contact too

RALPH WALDO EMERSON. 139

anæmic, ended by praising its spirituality.
And in his presence, the most conscientious
may give way to the natural and honourable
impulse which compels us to praise without
discrimination the great servers of mankind.

He believed persistently in the practise of
expressing the thought with the pen.

"Write, write," he was wont to say to me;
"there is no way to learn to write except by
writing."

There was a young Rousseau—I knew him
well—who devoted years to the preparation
of a psychological novel, which our Antinous
had counselled writing out at length, though
the result could not well be otherwise than
it was—a mass of worthless manuscript.
Although he knew well how vast is the
number of books brought to be printed in
comparison with the few that are, yet he
never disgusted the would-be author with
such statistics or discouraged effort, but
always considered the satisfaction of expression a sufficient final result.

It is given to all men of letters to love the
hermit habit; but Mr. Emerson's extreme
solitariness was dictated from afar.

"I hope you like walks alone and in by-
paths. You find your best muse there," said

he to me; and the powers that conspired to
build him, the manes of seven generations
spoke in the expression.

He avoided cities even when abroad,
seeking always, when he could, some quiet
thorp wherein to disappear; liked not his
wife's (Mrs. Lidian's) home, because it was a
larger village than Concord, and—the statement is veracious, not authentic—was thankful
when the inclemency of the weather assisted
his own retirement. Even thence he frequently
dwelt apart. He did some work on Monad-
nock, and in the Old Manse. "Nature"
came from one of these remote, hidden
studies.

"But I find my best working solitude," he
said to me, "in some New York hotel or
country inn, where no one knows or can find
me. There one finds one's self."

In his walks he was inquisitive, would
interrupt the subject to remark upon anything
uncommon; especially objects meretricious
or false rarely escaped his surveillant eye.
It was a marvel that an attention so inward
could also be so outward. A wooden building made to imitate brick or stone, painted
blinds where were no real ones, ashlar work,
false façades, fences of wood made to re-

semble iron, any object suggestively untrue
annoyed him.

One day I called upon him, to find him
copying. The next day and the next,—he
was still copying. It was necessary for some
purpose, he explained, that he should possess
some sixty pages of manuscript in duplicate.
I offered to relieve him; but he said he must
do this, as he was forced to do everything, for
himself.

I like to recall such facts as these, because
continental critics have stated that he bor-
rowed Montaigne, imitated the Orientalists
and Germans; and these are not the traits
of a borrowing man. To me, Emerson's
swift convictions, his sunniness and fidelity
to the homely sincerities, are not even of like-
ness to Montaigne's pedantic and desultory
earthliness, and his unforsaken whims. I have
not seen any direct citations to substantiate
these charges. They have never appeared in
domestic latitudes, and I do not think they
could have been made by persons acquainted
with Mr. Emerson, or familiar with his work;
for he shrank from appropriating anything
not originally his, or that had not been
assimilated by his own mental character. He
would rather be a kitten and cry " mew," and

that mew would be Emerson's. It is true he sought the Oriental literature, as did Carlyle the German. Emerson imported it for Americans. Who among us knew of the Vedas or Ramáyana until he scattered the desire for them here and there as a household treasure ? And who has sought Saadi or Hafiz but has encountered a disappointment of hopes based on Emerson's richer page, to whom the impossibility of even a moment's masquerade or carrying foreign colours for the most transient purposes was ancestral? The same virility and rarity of organization which has made him so eminent, has forced others of the same unreceptive blood into successes, as marked in commercial and professional pursuits. His life and revealings were his own and explicit.

Openness to conversion is, perhaps, as admirable as firmness of conviction, but less suggestive of a severe individuality. Mr. Emerson's methods were positive. He did not deny. That he never disclosed impatience when his positions were traversed led some to believe that he held his doctrines with a light hand. But once I heard him defend assailed statements ; and that occasion afforded a remarkable instance of the tenacity with which he held his views, and the cogency with which

he could advocate them. He listened so well,
extended such appreciative consideration, and
then there was such an apparent yielding in
the fairness of his returns, that no one was prepared for the discovery, until it was inevitable
from the larger view he presented, that confusion must follow those who withstood him. He
did not compromise, nor did he proclaim ; but
his quiet rejoinders concealed the dark fires of
volcanic regions which catch where they are
not seen. It was from his example a brief
and gentle discussion—a heated magnet loses
its power—and not abandoned until all saw
that there was positively no hope of eliminat-
ing from such pertinacity any position once
assumed. But the charm consisted in the
quiet reappearance of the arraigned propositions ; they came clad always in new
language, with illustrations that gave them
a new force, but the same indestructible
identity. I can never remember the incident
without applying to it quite as much as to the
divinity of existence the old Brahma lines :—

> " If the red slayer thinks he slays,
> Or if the slain think he is slain,
> They know not well the subtle ways
> I keep and pass and turn again." *

---

* A good instance is this quatrain of Mr. Emer-

But, *marchons*, I touch a single subor-
dinate feature too long for faithfulness.
Polemicism was foreign to Mr. Emerson.
His opponents wove his sisal fibres into
ropes, but when they were drawn tight he
had escaped. All of him the attitude of
hostility could detain was the linen cloth
about the body. He would not do battle for
his precepts ; he did not wish followers, nor
was he an iconoclast. The images are re-.
moved or burned after, not by him. He
looked upon all men as individuals who would
sometime become thoughtful, and was content if he could hasten the process. Moreover, he was deeply sensitive to the many-
sidedness of truth, and the impossibility of
uttering in regard to it the complete word.

How this contrasts with the bold and
stormy Carlyle! With what tempests of
humour that, as Emerson said, "floated
everything," the great Scotchman would
sweep opposition away ; or, quite as likely,

son's resurrecting power. Compare Krishna's song
in the Bhagavad-Gita, Edwin Arnold's translation :—

" He who shall say, 'Lo ! I have slain a man,'
He who shall think, 'Lo ! I am slain !' those both
Know naught ! Life cannot slay. Life is not
    slain ! "

with what electrical violence he would destroy
it !

They were always at war, their methods
transverse, and their separations pronounced.
Carlyle's advantage was in force, Emerson's
in insight. His feet were always on the
earth. And so he believed in the grandeur
of the masses and their self-originated ad-
vancement, while Carlyle's sympathies were
never democratic. "A great deep cliff,"
he said, "divides us, in our ways of practically looking at this world." Emerson
told me that Carlyle was impatient for him
to know Goethe—a knowledge which did
much less for the American than for the
Scotchman. Both encouraged genuine
comers, but neither could tolerate insincerity,
which they destroyed, one with lightning,
and the other with light.

But I hasten to my vicissitudes with Mr.
Emerson's literature; for they traversed mis-
understandings with his methods to which
every young and new reader is exposed.
For many years before I saw him his pages
seemed to me immortal. They stirred me
as a Bible; so completely (according to my
capacity) did I receive their revelation, so
keenly did I feel their bracing and severe

L

climate; the fine exhilaration they create; their insight; their sententious wisdom; the nobility of their character. So the highest aspirations of my mind were met and satisfied. Then I was disturbed by bruit of under-meanings and tones that I had not caught. I learned that I ought to find a series of sub-conscious, logical links, subtly binding these inspirations into an integral whole; and that they were inhabited by a double interior sense, like that attributed to Swedenborg by his disciples. I had been for months passionately and patiently absorbed in the search when Mr. Emerson himself came upon the scene. "Now," I exclaimed, "that I can see the master, I shall be taught."

Well do I remember the charmed afternoon that he put into my hands one of his personal collections,—I do not know their name; Emersoniana, I called them, gatherings which had grown from year to year until they would make a volume; original reflections, extracts with pen and pencil, scraps, personal draughts, and even a gallery of words and brilliant and studious expressions; like Bacon's "Promus," anything and everything that had formed a mental experience for him. Here and there were isolated

quantities of manuscript, evidently denoting
what he had meditated, and studies of particular subjects with his own commentaries.
He obviously had sipped from books rather
than read; and these repertories witnessed
that he had obeyed his own maxim to " shut
the book when your own thought comes."
It seemed as if he had preserved everything,
whether in good form or not; but this was a
mistake; for he destroyed much that should
have been spared. Many of the passages I
at once recognized as friends of the rostrum.
In a moment it flashed upon me that I was
in the presence of one of the manuscript
sources of the addresses, essays, treatises,
yea, the books themselves. So soon as I
could realize this, I sought to pursue through
a few of the pages the theme on which they
advertised to discourse. But I very soon
became unable to trace connections. Here
was the subject, looked at, looked about,
looked into; but here, as well, were others
remotely relevant or not relevant at all, and
paragraphed bits of print, pen-illustrations,
adages, criticisms ingenious and delicate
reflections obviously just as they came, and
on anything—and then the subject again
appearing, like the uncalculated return of a

comet. The orbit was long, and an ellipse.
I went back and over the ground again and
again with scrutinizing eyes, but I could
not be mistaken, and finally gave it up,
convinced that the wigwam was lost, not the
Indian.

Studying still closer into the construction
of the propositions themselves, it became
plain that Mr. Emerson considered the
paragraph for him the limit of logical expression. He tried to crowd everything into
it; an attempt which the following one
exposed. These fragmentary and unrelated
statements produced upon me an impression
of isolation, and gave an air of incomplete-
ness. With their drastic quality and weight,
they overpowered the narrative. So since
have our gigantic Californian sequoias made
me indifferent as to the trend or extent of
the forest they constitute. The thoughts
seemed islanded, as he said, "paragraphs
incompressible, each sentence an infinitely
repellent particle." And Carlyle's descrip-
tion: "By-the-by, I ought to say the sentences are very *brief*, and did not, in my
sheet reading, always entirely cohere for me.
Pure genuine Saxon; strong and simple; of
a clearness, of a beauty,—but they did not

sometimes rightly stick to their foregoers and
their followers; the paragraphs not as a
beaten ingot, but as a beautiful *bag of duck
shot* held together by canvas" (Carlyle: Letter
to Emerson, November 3, 1844). And one
remembers Theodore Parker's comparison of
Mr. Emerson's sentences to an army all
officers; but they are advancing on a long
march.

And now I thought I understood better
about the frequent lapse and hiatus in the
Lyceum appearances and the lectures as
published, which frequently bewilder the
young student. Mr. Emerson sought not
occasions, and determined not to write for
them; but in his position he could not avoid
them, nor could he lift bodily into them the
original fabric of his work without some con-
cession to time and place; and Bronson
Alcott has drawn a picture of Mr. Emerson
on his knees in his study, trying to piece
together for such exigency sheets of written
matter with which the floor was carpeted.
But art is inflexible, and there were audacious
chasms which even his carpentry could not
join, and which had been abandoned in
despair. This physiological connection, I
fear, must be accepted rather than the

psychological; but any logical construction
would sever those tendons which God never
joined together. So I no longer wondered
at the hesitant turning of leaves which had
characterized the lecturing. What trying
moments some of those pages must have
occasioned; what temporary embarrassment,
incident upon extracting anything consecu-
tive from them! Well, I knew now why no
lecture was twice alike; for, lo, the theme
occupied many hours, and we got only one.
Here before me was the original body, without form, though I could almost see the
creator's hand moving on the manuscript's
face! As for a hidden sense, I said (and
this conclusion remains unchanged), the
readers who find one in Faust may in
Emerson; but they will find it as the cup
was found in Benjamin's sack, and by a
similar process.

The next step toward possession of my
author was a most important one, namely,
my introduction to Plato and Coleridge. I
found myself returned by them to the same
posture of attention Emerson had originally
excited. The Socratic dialogues, especially,
while apparently lawless, exhibited that
nothing important was omitted in the ground

gone over; and I discovered that there was really the same progress as if the manikin process had been pursued, and the argument anatomized. These imaginary conversations, and Coleridge's discursive discussions, became to me object-lessons disclosing Emerson's secret of advancing by a natural instead of the artificial order I had been trained in. Then I recalled what he had taught me (" Counsel "), to permit no ratiocinative steps to appear, and I saw how foolish it had been in me to suppose that he would permit them to appear himself.

"Why could it not be," I asked myself, "that he dispenses with the syllogism, which is rather a form of stating proof than proving, and performs his reasoning in quiet, acquainting the reader only with the epigrammatic results; and that these limited diversions, given with such excess of candor that they cause me to be over-solicited by them, really exhibit the author's truth by the exhaustion of exits from it?" Applying this dialectic to the " Essays," I was delighted to find that they were responsive to it, and displayed under it the same intelligent plan as that unquestioningly acknowledged in his more concrete work, like " Nature," " English

Traits," his orations, and his campaign
addresses, which march like a phalanx.
From this point of view, there is one axis
through the main portion of his writings;
and I regard them also as an exhibition of
what, in the best sense, natural methods of
composition can accomplish in the way of
style, to the construction of which he never
gave a thought, and so produced one entirely
new and fascinating, characterized by insight
rather than argument; seizing truths and
presenting them without the effort, hitherto
common, of showing relations and connections. That Mr. Emerson's friends have
generally not been content with this accomplishment, and have sought to conform him
to the old rules and ways, I regard as unfortunate.

No new vogue gains permanent admiration
unless it is congenial to an unrecognized
necessity and the natural vehicle of its
creator. That adopted by Mr. Emerson
appears to me to be a vindication alike of
his sagacity and his conscientiousness. It
was peculiarly adapted to the time of its
appearance, and to the man whose first work
was to break the heavy equilibrium amid
which he found himself; to agitate into life

the settled New England torpor, and with the intellectual activity to attain higher moral processes. There remained one step farther in this determination of method.

The reader of Mr. Emerson encounters (often introduced by the formula, " I have heard," or, " as a certain poet sang ") utterances that are fragments of a spiritual philosophy or vision of which we have not the entire substance. The altitudes from which these verities come is beyond that sought by the thinker or poet ; it is in the region of that of the seer. The genesis of these thoughts of God is quite as much the experiences of his sinless life as the intuitions of his highest and mystic moments, when the universe became self-revelatory. The spiritual character of these themes forbids their approach by the methods of empirical logic ; but in their presence there is a profound and central self-containment. A large unity and integrity resembling that of Nature (within whose content are surprises and contrasts) is in all expressions of the Over-Soul or Supreme Reality, and they are in it " as the ocean is in the bucket and the bucket in the ocean."

I submit this elementary record to the

young and new reader of Emerson, in the
hope that it may be of some help in deter-
mining the question whether his presentation
is within scientific form.

An organic philosophy he did not offer.
His claim was that there is nothing complete.
The clement Parcæ in his study, who were
ever spinning a fairer thread, presided over
his mental attitude, which always said, All
objects are unknowable on account of their
relativity. Nothing is concluded here or can
be. I utter the final word on no subject.
How different this from Beecher's study, for
instance, where the great circular work-wheel
and chair in the centre somehow always presented positive and final declaration. But
Emerson would weave no completed fabric.
Far be it from him to dogmatize or insist
upon any pronouncement as complete or
final. He said what he saw, and as far as
he saw, without reasoning and without logical
unfolding. Facts, yes; but let the reader do
his own dreaming, and make his own com-
pletions. His reward does not depend on
solidarity which is often artificial.

"Do not put hinges to your work to make
it cohere," he once said in substance to me.
And we must remember that through such

joints much sophistry has crept into the
world. Sincerity was Mr. Emerson's soul;
and he unhesitatingly preferred lack of con-
tinuity to the least ambiguity regarding intention. Classification for the sake of external
order and system was unnatural to him. Nor
was he sensitive to their absence in Carlyle,
whose writings are a congeries of magnificent
contradictions. It may be that this temperament in Mr. Emerson asserted itself at times
too strongly for his wish or his work, as certainly did his reluctance from severe thought.
After his proposition had once attained form
and been passed upon, it must remain. If
the next could be made to harmonize with it,
well; if not, the next must look out for itself;
it, too, must be true, or it would not be here.

These omissions and silences in Emerson's
literature reward, and it is well to master its
cipher. It is the way a poet writes. Emerson
was essentially a poet, and the essays are
lyric and a solvent force. No one reads
them, any more than he would a book of
poems, by quantity.

"A poet does not say to mankind, This,
and this only, is true, and you will find it
consistent with every other truth I proclaim.
He says, I feel this, at this moment, to be

true; so much of the living world I can portray you. You ask sincerity of utterance from the poet, not systematic thinking. Here and there flash across the mind unmistakable truths or generous sentiments, which, surely, it is well to utter, though in a partial and disjointed manner. There is a certain freedom of utterance allowed to the poet which is denied to the prose writer, for this very reason—that he is not expected to follow out to its last logical result every opinion and sentiment he expresses."

As regards the poetic form, what fetter Mr. Emerson's genius felt from the rules of art, or within what limits his temperament confined his inspirations, we cannot know; but we have from a most conscientious critic, himself a poet, in regard of Mr. Emerson the judgment: "If he had been frequently sustained at heights he was capable of reaching, he would unquestionably have been one of the sovereign poets of the world." But what poet has inhabited such heights long?

To me the graces that transcend in Mr. Emerson's poetry are, with this spiritual elevation, its allusiveness and infectious individualism—that quality which constrained Carlyle to write him that his anonymous

work was at once distinguishable in a mis-
cellaneous gathering of writings. But in the
poetry, as in the prose, the *laissez faire*
atmosphere, necessarily noticeable, was found
exasperating.; and his critics crowded the
columns of the Boston and New England press
at times with attack, but found in them no
word of answer. Even the Archons of
literary opinion raised their deep and seldom
voices in vain. He was out and away from
the cry of the hounds.

One other of the deep lessons that con-
fronted me from those precious manuscript
pages of the master belongs here ; and that
was the evidences of painstaking and labour,
of careful reconsideration and retouching of
the form which were everywhere. Countless
of these memoranda were pasted or pinned
together, the language changed and rechanged
until the paper resembled palimpsist, and the
thoughts like sheet metal rolled and ham-
mered to the smallest possible compass. A
severer judge of himself never wrote. What
a rebuke to those writers who "throw off"
on the spur of the moment! Nothing that he
did was "thrown off." Immense was the
tributary study, deep and long the meditation,
well brooded were all statements ; but, more

than all, how firmly, with what infinite
patience, was the expression manipulated,
especially in his fine use of the common
everyday words which find on his page
their apotheosis, and approve him a great
master of English ! Here and there on inter-
jected leaves I could even trace the history
of a sentence from the first free and mordant
enunciation through modifications, abate-
ments, and restrictions to narrower outline,
then tempered to the exact fact, and the clean
and clear distinctions, the

"River to streamlet reducing, and mountain to slope
    subduing."

Drop by drop the enchantment was distilled
which changed the water into wine. It is
this fine and full control of his instrument
which confers such a subtle charm on his
books, gives them their lucidity and surprise,
and makes of them English classics. Truly
a sayer was Emerson. Sometimes the pem-
mican process has been too rigid, and one
regrets the parsimony of words. But always,
if you repeat what he says, it must be in his
own language, even when he uses "reliable,"
"loan," as a verb, "isolate" as an adjective,
"party" for individual, "the three first," etc.
    He claimed that the best statement scanned

and cited, "Let there be light, and there
was light." And we know of the lines—

" I heard, or seemed to hear, the chiding sea
Say, ' Pilgrim, why so late and slow to come?' "

that they were substantially originally written
as prose. Expression to him was a sensuous
delight, and so his sentences are keen of
flavour, delicious, and refreshing. He tasted
his words. Who has said as perfectly those
things which are difficult to say at all? He
told me that he was not well when he could
not write, and in the study he had infinite
patience. He even suspected his fervours,
and it took him a long time to secure in his
spirited paragraphs their wide, and at the
same time their carefully distinctive meaning.
This needful elaboration perhaps explains
his epistolary defect. Any necessitated spontaneity embarrassed him, and he was forced
to copy his letters and search apparent ease
of composition. Once in my room he said—
   " I see you have many gathered volumes
of correspondence of distinguished men and
women. It is a fortune to write good letters.
I do not have it. I do not love letter-
writing, and do not write letters readily."
   So his few apparently offhand public
addresses did not come pat, but on two

occasions at least within my knowledge there were manuscripts behind. He was not equal to the exigent demand, the immediate divination and mastery of impulse. And the genesis of thought in the presence of an audience, revealing to them that they were in some wise the parent of it, which made Beecher and Phillips, for instances, so popular, was a perpetual surprise to him. I cannot think of Emerson as envying anything; but this extempore knack tempted him. So a friend relates of him that one day, coming out of a crowded audience which he had disappointed in the middle of his address by mislaying some pages of his manuscript (so distressing him that he took his seat), and which Phillips had immediately delighted with his oration, Mr. Emerson said—

" I would give a thousand shekels for that man's secret."

So he said of Beecher, *àpropos* of his oratory in England during the war—

" What will you do with an eloquent man ? He makes you laugh, and you cannot throw your egg."

These statements disclose an estimate of eloquence coincident with the ordinary one, rather than with his definition given in

"Counsel." Accepting that definition which was perhaps temperamental, he was almost incomparably eloquent.

He conveys little in regard to the fine arts, painting, statuary, or even music. I do not think these addressed him. Neither are the exact sciences represented as having received attention. Indeed, of mathematics, Mr. Emerson said to me in my home—

"Some mathematical works here, too. What hours of melancholy mine cost! It was long before I learned that there is something wrong with a man's brain who loves them."

Such remarks as these emphasize that Mr. Emerson hoped to help less by demonstration and reasoning than by breaking up apathy and imparting impulse; and who that has brooded over Emerson's writings and felt their fascination, spontaneous as if from an improvisatore, salient with all the qualities of suggestiveness and motive-power, with imagination and intuition instead of syllogisms, and words of a fine vitality coercing into new, strange, and eruptive moods,—but has felt that he has before him an illustration of what the English language, unaided by action, can achieve in moving the souls of men?

M

MANHOOD.

MANHOOD.

THIS is the story of an enthusiasm. One who comes to the long leisure of youth in its arid but most auspicious days, concentrates its vague and restless aspirations and nourishes its heart, takes possession with an exclusiveness proportioned to the service. Not learning or wisdom or personal appearance and fascinations create these profound and permanent impressions. When they are asked for, the inquisition is deeper. What is the differentiating substance, the inner quality, the central and essential character of the man himself? for that we conjure the invisible angel who has conquered us by his audacious touch. No observations and calculations of shadows to determine altitude will avail. We can only know the man by the affections, which, as Wordsworth says in a noble passage, are their own justification.

So I knew him, and yet knew him not. For that is the nobility of every great man, that he cannot be divined, but sends the seeker farther and farther into his own unsurveyed heavens. So he was incommensurable, and might have been taken for the pneuma Plato celebrated, who can see two sides of a thing; only, so far from being simple, he was many-sided. His resemblances were of Socrates, Buddha, and Ben Franklin; but he continually surprised and eluded.

How often as young men, before we had ever seen him, we used to gather about the study table in those earlier days before his coming, and create him mechanically from his books! How little were our verbatim imaginations prepared for the propensities we encountered! We went out to see one who had forsworn all luxuries, a man of abstemious and austere habit and severest standard. We never found him.

Well I remember now the anxious consultation and miserable misgivings over our little banquet to him! Long we hesitated over the items of the simple order to the village caterer! His country resources afforded ice-cream and comfits! But had not our guest in his published writings for-

bidden them, except for those who dare not
trust the entertainment of their own minds?
And I venture the guess that neither of us
have since experienced that peculiar creep of
surprise and relief that gradually stole over
us as we saw (though, ignorantly, our repast
was offered at an hour when the stomach
should be sacred of intrusion, three p.m.)
our dainties disappear with an appetite we
had supposed characteristic only of under-
graduates.

So, again, on the road, when he would
stop wayfarers and inquire about the pro-
prietors of certain estates, and praise their
thrift and enterprise, remembering how I had
kindled reading his eloquent advocacy of a
renunciation "of the premature comforts of
an acre, house, and barn to traverse the star-
lit deserts of truth!" I felt that I did not
understand him—that, in boy's parlance, his
words meant one thing and he another.

Of course this was the boy's stupidity.
Our eyes, myopic and level only to the
plinth, could not take in what it upheld or
represented. But, after all, has not the
blunder been shared by older and harder
heads? When the master's presence was
missed from the company of Pythagoreans

and herb-eaters at Brook Farm and Fruit-
lands, and when advocates of special reform,
attached by the encouraging hospitality of
his writings, sought his espousal of their
schemes in vain, was it not apparent that
they, too, must take his words as parole?

Then there are in his literature intuitions
which logic seems to continually overcome,
positions which are easily shown to be apparently unreconcilable.

And one is reminded of what he says of
Plato. " The dearest defenders and disciples
are at fault. One man thinks he meant this,
and another that. He said one thing in one
place, and the reverse of it in another place.
He argues on this side and on that. Indeed,
admirable texts can be quoted on both sides
of every great question from him " (Emerson
on Plato, but on himself as well).

Farthermore, he advertises of himself:
" But lest I would mislead any, when I have
my own head and obey my own whims, let
me remind the reader that I am only an
experimenter. Do not set the least value on
what I do, or the least discredit on what I
do not do, as if I pretended to settle anything
as true or false. I unsettle all things. No
facts are to me sacred, none are profane. I

simply experiment, an endless seeker, with no past at my back " (" Circles ").

Now such words as these, and such experiences as those just narrated, have served to puzzle and deter new seekers. But to the true Emersonian, the facts indicated by these words occasion no unrest. So far from having this effect, they are recognized as being from the master's inner self. He would unsettle all things, why? That we should pursue them. He will have no sacred facts. Why? That we should look all facts in the face. And this is the open secret of his power to-day. Others give us themselves. He gives and maintains to us ourselves, our best selves. We do not seek him for knowledge, but for wisdom, and the best wisdom—a new life. And it is this universal search that indicates that seminal, germinal, developing quality which is the central essence of the man himself. He comes immediately into the mind, a revolutionary force, questioning, suggesting, destroying composure, provoking doubt of the order that is, destroying gods whether Penates or Empyrean, not with blows, but with frost and fire, emancipating thought, sowing a sane discontent and elation; then stimulator, inspirer, liberator of power. And

with what other service is such service com·
parable? To this temper he was ever constant. Even in his old age, which is not
seldom the obscuration of genius, when his
days became almost merely loitering and
literary, he still kept this native bravery,
and I believe refers to it when he says he
obeyed

" The voice at eve obeyed at prime."

And so to the heart of youth I would say :
He comes especially to you. You will find
these days everybody quoting him, and not a
few praising. While he was too wise to seek
the inculcation of an harmonized system of
all truth, yet no one has given us so many
and such rare truths. No one in these con-
gested days will yet guide you so well to
those heights where are the *jodel* and the
edelweiss. But not for this does he come to
you. It is the invigorating, elevating soul of
him that you must meet. You, too, will go
in search of it ; you, too, will be impelled by
his words ; and you, too, are called upon to
forepoint at your peril when they are born
of his imagination, his mood, his uplifting
genius, his intuition, as well as when their
source is his valid commonsense. He ex-
pects of you that you will obey the placard,

"Private way, no thoroughfare," hung by this verger over the turns of the quadrangle. He, himself, the

> " Musketaquit, goblin strong,
>   Of shard and flint makes jewels gay.
>   They lose their grief who hear his song,
>   And where he winds is day of day."

His are the loftiest conceptions, those which do the most to make us discontented with the ordinary and commonplace, and by that token are essentially incapable of being literally translated into speech or personified in action. So you will find his words always wise, always true. Follow Emerson's utterances chronologically from the first obscure but stimulative manifestation of his spirit, when he had not yet come to the full knowledge of his purpose, but was conscious mainly of the necessity of thawing out the climate, through to his later lifetime, when his philosophy forms an unbroken fringe falling in separate threads of beauty and use that touch at all points wisely and sanely our humanity. I read a portion of the essays to an old farmer. He clapped his hands, and exclaimed that whoever wrote that book knew how to "farm it." Yet the characteristic admired was merely that of practically a holding to

the fact by prehensility of tail—a valuable
trait even if simial, but one so common
that it would not distinguish. The soar of
the first gospel is necessary to lift the last.
Those primal pages are to be reverently
treasured by the Emersonian because they
first drew us to him. Indeed, the earlier
idealism, the era of the doctrine of Transcendentalism and its accompanying intima-
tions, finds its interpretation in the later,
warmer, and riper work; as, in the Arctic
traveller's mythus, the speech congealed to
the hearers of his own time became audible
in after-days. How much to us has been
and will be ever the high sentences of that
earlier manhood, and his inability to conform, which was to the Jews a stumbling-
block and to the Greeks foolishness! We
would not miss the records of him in the
matter of the Lord's Supper, Public Prayer,
Christening, etc., even though later in life it
may be that he would not have called these
forms sensualizing, nor have failed to find
some hands other than Channing's pure.
enough to touch the forehead of the "hya-
cinthine boy."

The moral quality of his genius was not
less its unfailing characteristic. The man

stood behind or abreast of his every statement, and it came clothed with dignity from
his sincerity. Great events moved him deeply.
At their approach, his other worldliness and
pure speculations were put one side; and
all low motives, considerations of mere ex-
pediency that had been mixed with the
question, vanished in his strong presence
as if themselves purely speculative. Witness
his earliest advocacy of political reform; his
expostulations with President van Buren;
and in the Bell-Everett matter his voice,
which was the conscience of New England;
his foremost abolition pulpit; his and
William Lloyd Garrison's anti-slavery apostle-
ship; his noble address at Concord on the
death of Lincoln; his emancipation speeches,
with their lava fire. In these was the voice
of the over-soul, his God through him. We
have no more momentous manifestation of
the national spirit more free from the ferocity
of his colleagues, more timely and weighty.
As befitted an epoch-originating man, he
was above the atmospheric envelope, and
not affected by its disturbances, but spoke
from the calm heights where gathered and
for ever will gather with him the noble and
victorious of all eras. The tone of loyalty to

the commonwealth always commanded his respect and forbade his criticism. Once, when an audience at which a friend was present, was compelled to listen to an individual who persisted in reading some screed on national politics, Mr. Emerson broke the silence that followed the infliction with the one word of praise—"Patriotic!"

But this recognizing the best possible was a quality always transparent in him. His preference was persistent for only the good in the human life around him, and he would have nothing to do with its lemurs. Melancholy was a chimpanzee trait to him. He rejoiced in Fuller's maxim, "An ounce of cheerfulness is worth a pound of sadness to serve God with." He had not the capacity to form even a recognizing acquaintance with the darker facts in human character. Undoubtedly, his faith in its reactions was extreme. He perhaps gifted it with some qualities it did not possess; and it may be there were some chasms he walked over with buoyant step because with bandaged eyes; or was it that they were too intently fixed on the zenith to see the nadir?

He fought with the bright battalions. And

their allies of the graver faiths have proclaimed that his serenity of optimism invalidated his authority as a practical moral exponent; while even many of his friends have feared that the natural enamel was too protective which kept him so stainless. His Greek absorption of the beautiful and the delicacy of his spiritual organization may go some way toward a sanction which with difficulty is sought in his own instructor, Nature, whose processes and penalties are darkly luminous with the presence of a principle very like that of evil. Whether here the linden leaf fell on Siegfried is a question which time will answer. I believe that his changeless disregard of the vast power of the will to destroy the ideal nature in man has its source in the great hope which inspired that noble question, "Who can set limits to the remedial force of the Spirit?" What voice, even to an age so facilely incurious of its own dark problems and so unconscious of sin as this, has a stronger moral imperative and from a higher plane of religious motive than that of him who beyond question was the greatest vindicator and exalter of the soul the new world has seen?

There are those who believe that he saw

clearly because he did not feel keenly, that within he was emotionless, his sympathies being rather with abstract humanity. But all that is noble in the human heart is accosted by, and greets him. His love was for the man in the man; and that love, with his instinctive knowledge of the central secrets of being, was the source of his power. From it his influence exhaled as perfume from a flower. But the inner tenderness is disclosed in such expression as the following to Carlyle :—

"I write to implore you to be careful of your health. You are the property of all whom you rejoice in heart and soul, and you must not deal with your body as your own. O my friend, if you would come here, and let ᵛme nurse you and pasture you in my nook of this long continent, I will thank God and you therefor morning and evening, and doubt not to give you, in a quarter of a year, sound eyes, round cheeks, and joyful spirits."

And how Mrs. Carlyle wrote him : "Friend, who years ago, in the Desert, descended on us, out of the clouds as it were, and made one day there look like enchantment for us, and left me weeping that it was only one day."

It is because these memories and such

unpermitted memories as these are so near
the heart, because his volitions were so pure
and his demeanour so lowly, that we return
to these things; and, remembering him less
as a man of unmatched originality, an unfailing fountain of delightful ideas, a moral
genius of extraordinary insight and mastery,
an architect of new horizons, a generative
and elemental power even, than as an inheritance of the divine presence, think of him
lastingly and lovingly with the Scripture,
"Some shall not sleep, but be changed."

THE END.

PRINTED BY WILLIAM CLOWES AND SONS, LIMITED,
LONDON AND BECCLES.

N